CAKE POPS
and COFFEE

A New Conversation
About Trauma

*how to laugh, cry, and
love your whole story*

Katie Maloney

DISCLAIMER: It is acknowledged that the **Save for Later Box** and **Meet Your Selves** techniques offered in the *Let's Get Some Tools* section of this book are based on therapeutic EMDR techniques originally learned by the author in her own process with therapy and are not proprietary creations of the author.

Cake Pops and Coffee:

A New Conversation About Trauma - How Laugh, Cry, and Love Your Whole Story

Copyright © 2019 by Katie Maloney

The content of this book is for general informational purposes only. It is not meant to be used, nor should it be used, to diagnose or treat any medical condition or to replace the services of your physician or other healthcare provider. The advice and strategies contained in the book may not be suitable for all readers.

Neither the author, publisher, nor any of their employees or representatives guarantees the accuracy of information in this book or its usefulness to a particular reader, nor are they responsible for any damage or negative consequence that may result from any treatment, action taken, or inaction by any person reading or following the information in this book.

For permission requests or to contact the author, visit:
www.katiemaloneycoaching.com

ISBN-13: 978-0-578-60879-2

PRINTED IN THE UNITED STATES OF AMERICA

To Bri, for sticking with me through everything.

Tammy, who believed in me unconditionally.

And for anyone who mistakenly thought this was a cookbook, but kept reading anyway.

Don't Skip This Part

For years, I felt a greatness inside of me—a power I knew could make all of my dreams come true. I knew that I was capable of living the life I always wanted. I knew I could step into a career that felt truly aligned with my life's purpose, purchase the home of my dreams, meet a truly loving partner, become abundantly financially stable, and finally start purchasing toilet paper from somewhere other than the dollar store down the street from my apartment. #Goals.

But something always stopped me. It took me a long time to realize that the something was me. I was the one holding myself back. It was all my bullshit—the self-doubts, negative beliefs, fears, memories, and everything else that developed from the trauma I experienced. I knew that I had the capacity to live my greatest life, and I knew that all I had to do to unlock that potential was start working through the layers of the abuse I experienced plus all the cruddy mental stuff that came along with it. The only problem was, I didn't know how to do that.

So, I looked to books for help. But the only books available about trauma were either psychology books that made me feel like a social experiment or depressingly titled self-help books that made me feel like a wounded puppy. Before I even opened the books, I could feel the weight of the topics falling from the pages and suffocating me with mocking whispers saying, "Girl, you are irrevocably messed up." Okay, maybe that's a little overdramatic.

What I mean to say is, yes, I was sexually abused for the first eighteen years of my life. And yes, obviously, those experiences were terrible. But my story includes far more than just trauma. I laugh. I draw too much attention to myself on the dance floor at weddings (debatable). I cry during Subaru commercials that feature happy families making smores around a campfire. I hang out with friends. I get way more aggressive with people in my car than I ever would with someone face-to-face. I have beautiful, lighthearted, meaningful, funny, significant moments in my life every day, and I needed a book that included those moments, too.

I wanted to read something that felt like having a conversation with a trusted friend. I wanted to eat cake pops, drink coffee, and normalize casual conversation about abuse. I wanted a book that said we could cry when we need to and laugh when we want to. My friend, the book, would say, "Look, I experienced abuse, too, and I can tell you firsthand that you have everything you need inside of you. I hereby bestow upon you all the tools to overcome your abuse and unlock your full potential as the true warrior goddess you are."

Okay, maybe that's a little much. Really, I just wanted someone to say, "Look, I get how you're feeling. Try doing this and see if it helps." I needed a book that talks about LIVING after trauma—truly living.

So, I wrote that book. Here it is. I'm sharing the whole story of trauma—the difficult and the beautiful. I am going to get very real about how I made myself small because of negative beliefs that made me afraid of being seen. I am going to talk about saving my past selves and learning how to find safety within myself. I am going to share how I learned to masturbate in a way that transformed my perception of pleasure. I am going to talk about navigating relationships and sharing my past with my partners. I am sharing how I cut through all the bullshit that resulted from the abuse I experienced and how I learned to step into my power, love myself, and truly live after trauma.

In sharing my story, I hope I can inspire you to do the same. So, let's get some cake pops and coffee and share some stories.

CONTENTS

Let's Get Some *Tools*

My heart is pounding as I stand in front of the building, about to ring the doorbell. The hood of my coat is pulled over my face so that she can't see me on the security cameras, and my sister is hiding in the bushes on the side of the building.

"Here we go," I say as I press the bell. A moment passes but it feels like days before the buzzer goes off, signaling that the door is now unlocked. I quickly pull open the door and step inside. I hold the door open as my sister emerges from her hiding spot and runs in behind me.

"We're in," I say calmly, but my heart feels as if it is going to explode. I slowly walk up the steps to the front office, where I know she's working. My sister is right behind me. When we reach the top of the steps, I see her immediately. She is sitting at her desk. It's weird to see such a monstrous person in such a mundane setting. I pause. I don't say anything, I just look at her. She looks up from her desk and greets me warmly—again, a weird contrast to her true nature. She doesn't recognize me at first. It's been over five years since I've seen or talked with her.

"Hi," I say, and as her face changes from smiling to shock, I know she knows who I am.

I truly believe that, before we are born, our souls have a meeting of sorts with a bunch of other souls. They say, "Alright, here are the lessons Katie has to learn in her life and here are the souls who will help her live those lessons." Then, the souls all get together and choose who will play what part in our lives in order to set us up with the most opportunities to fulfill our life's purposes. For me, my life's purpose is to help people who have experienced trauma step into their true selves and power. In order to do that, my soul was assigned to live with the souls of my parents. Their souls and the abusive circumstances that I grew up in were the best available tools to teach me the lessons I needed in order to fulfill my life's purpose.

During the five years leading up to this meeting with my mother, I did all the self-work. I healed wounds, recognized and released old patterns, let go of negative beliefs, and truly moved forward from my past. But I never felt finished. I knew that the only way that my soul's connection with my mother would be complete and we could part ways forever would be for me to look her in the eyes and say, "I know what you and Dad did, and I forgive you."

"Do you want to talk here or outside?" I ask, fully prepared to unleash my entire speech in front of her coworkers.

"I'll be back," she says to a co-worker as she walks around her desk and meets us in the hallway. We don't say anything else yet. I begin walking down a hallway that leads outside. I can see the exit sign, but the walk feels like a 5k. I can feel the silence around us. I'm smiling. I suddenly realize that I'm not afraid. In fact, I am excited. I'm proud. I am here. I did the work and I made it to this moment. As we exit the building, I turn to face my mother.

"So, do you have anything to say?" I ask.

"Do I have anything to say?" she scoffs. "Katie, you're the one who showed up here. I have no idea what this is all about. All I know is that my children abandoned me…"

That's when I interrupt. "I know you sexually abused me and Sarah," I say.

My mother begins laughing. "What are you talking about?" she responds in the same way she did when she attempted to convince me I was crazy as a child.

I continue, "You drugged us every night and you watched as I was routinely raped by Dad, and you, yourself, sexually abused me and Sarah."

She scoffs again. I see in her eyes that there is nothing there.

"Why is it, that everything you remember is the truth, but I don't seem to remember any of this?" my mother asks, mockingly.

This time, I laugh. "You know, I have been asking myself the same question for years."

After five years of healing self-work, I felt ready to meet with my mother. I contacted the therapist I had worked with in high school and asked her to mediate the meeting. I contacted my mother via email and, surprisingly, she agreed to meet with me. I called off work, booked a flight, and spent the next two months preparing for the meeting. In addition to the things I wanted to say, I also had questions I wanted to ask. I believed that I needed to know the answers to these questions in order to truly heal from the abuse and move on. *Did you do things to prevent me from getting pregnant? Was there a group of people who you met with and allowed to ritually abuse us? Did you keep us in cages?* were just a few of the questions I had.

The night before we were supposed to meet, my mother emailed and canceled the meeting. She said that it was because she needed to protect herself after having children who "abandoned her and hurt her so deeply." I experienced the full spectrum of emotions at that moment. Put simply, I had a full-blown meltdown. After the tears subsided, my sister asked me how I wanted to move forward.

"I want to confront her at work," I replied.

"I want you to know that, despite the hell you put me through, and all the times you tried to convince me that I was unlovable, I have so many people in my life who love me. And I am capable of love. I love so many people, and I will continue doing so for the rest of my life," I say proudly. "You tried to pit me and Sarah against each other, but we love each other—look, we are here together. Everything you did couldn't stop us from loving each other.

"I know you were also a victim," I continue. "I know that your mom and your dad both sexually abused you." Then, the words flow more easily than I imagined they would, "I forgive you." I smile as Sarah and I begin walking away. Almost immediately, my mother begins yelling after us.

"I release you in light and love," I say, and it's over.

I am not going to pretend that everything was incredible after that. After the adrenaline of the moment wore off, my sister and I were left with the emotions that come from facing one of the most vile, abusive monsters in our life. Additionally, I couldn't shake the terrible feeling that I didn't get all the closure I was hoping I would get from that conversation. The adrenaline was too high and the conversation was too rushed for me to remember, let alone calmly read off, all the questions I had spent months compiling. *How would I ever get the answers? How could I ever really get closure without knowing the answers?* Then the thought popped into my head: *I have always known the answers to those questions.* They were just so terrible that it was difficult to believe. A part of me wanted to hear them validated. But what I really needed to learn was that I didn't need anyone else's answers to know the truth.

Despite the closure from that day, I am not completely free of thoughts about my upbringing. There are days that I remember more about the abuse, or think of something I could have said during that conversation and a part of me wants to go back and really lay into my mother the way I didn't do before. When I look back on that day, it's actually kind of shocking how calm and happy and completely free of anger I was when I was talking with her. In fact, I felt lighter than I had in a really long time. I realize that any anger I feel towards my mother or my father stems from the untrue thought that they took something away from me.

Sometimes, I feel they took away my childhood. My childhood was an eighteen-year-long nightmare. Sometimes, I feel they took away my ability to freely be intimate with someone. There are days I wish that I could just have sex with my partner or a stranger or simply masturbate without having to overcome so many emotional obstacles. Sometimes, I picture my beautiful, perfect little girl self and I am overcome with rage, thinking of all the tears and horror my parents caused her. But as I stood face-to-face with my mother that day, I realized that neither she nor my father took anything away from me. They couldn't. Despite their best efforts, they were never able to take away any part of me. I was always, and still am, so completely whole—every part of me is exactly in place.

Yes, they did terrible things that hurt me, but they were never able and will never be able to take even the smallest of pieces away from who I am. When I realized that, nothing about my parents or past mattered anymore. I stood looking at my mother. For a brief moment, I felt like I was going insane, because here I was, standing in front of a monster from my childhood, and I felt nothing but release and forgiveness. **I was free.**

I want you to be free, too, which is why I am excited to talk with you about the abuse I've experienced. I really am. I am excited to share stories, to laugh, cry, reflect, and find support with all of you. The hope that you will do the same with me as you continue to read excites me the most. That said, I just talked about wanting to ask my mother if I was kept in a cage as a child, so we're going to get real here.

The cry-with-you component is valid. I truly believe with all my heart that we can talk about abuse in an open, even lighthearted manner, but I also recognize that these conversations can bring up challenging memories and feelings. So, before we begin, let's develop a few tools we can use throughout the course of our sharing.

Side note: Before we do anything, I want to say *stop*. Because, if you are anything like me, you are already geared up to try and control everything. So *stop*. When you are doing any of the exercises in this book or reading any of the chapters or meditating, you are not responsible for making anything work. You are not responsible for controlling your mind or your emotions or your responses.

I remember walking into my therapist's office with absolute anxiety, thinking, "Okay, so when I get there, I need to have an open mind. I need to recognize if I am starting to suppress memories. I need to find a way to let go of fear. I need to find some way to be in the present but also remember all the things I want to talk about…" *blah, blah, blah, control everything, put all the responsibility on my shoulders, blah, blah, blah.*

Stop it! I love you so much. You do not have to do anything except show up. You opening this book and starting to read is you showing up—your subconscious, your body, your soul will take it from here. If you are having trouble focusing or your mind keeps drifting to other thoughts, that's okay. Just show up, let your mind do what it wants, and you will make progress.

Design Your Me Space

Having a conversation with your best friend is way more fun while curled up on a soft sofa with your favorite pillows and blanket. So, we're going to start our adventure together by creating that soft, safe, and cozy space. If you are reading this at home, grab your favorite cuddle-up materials - make a pillow fort, turn on your twinkle lights, snuggle up in your favorite blanket, brew some tea, light some candles, hang up that sexy cowboys calendar, put on your favorite music. If you are not home, just imagine this space. What does it smell like? What does it look like? Is there a sexy cowboys calendar? Most importantly, how does it feel? This is your Me Space. You are creating this space for yourself. Every part of it that makes you feel good, you've placed there. How powerful is that? Your Me Space is real life proof that safety, comfort, and that snuggle-up feeling is always available inside you.

So why are we creating a Me Space? Your Me Space is where you get to feel everything without fear. You can feel happy and never worry that someone will walk in and rain on that happiness. You can feel vulnerable or confused or afraid and know that you have the time and space to take deep breaths, reflect, and feel safe again. This is where I encourage you to read and work on the activities in this book. But it's also a place where you can come back to if you start to feel overwhelmed by memories or flashbacks or triggers. Whether your Me Space is a place at home or a mental picture, settle into that space and know that all the safety you've ever needed is in this space—it's in you.

Alright, now that we are all cuddled up in our Me Spaces, we're going to develop a tool for holding our thoughts.

Create Your "Save For Later Box"

Like I said before, there may be memories or feelings or thoughts that pop up or that you choose to process while reading this book. That is great! What's not great is feeling like you are carrying all of those memories and feelings and thoughts around with you every moment of the day. So, we are creating a box for you to place all of those thoughts into. Once you are finished reading for the day or if, at any time, a thought becomes overwhelming or you need to take a break, you can place the thought, feeling, or memory into your box to process later.

My box is actually a bowl—a beautiful, round glass bowl that exudes and is completely surrounded by bright white light. And I use my bowl all the time. It's especially great when I'm trying to go to bed but I can't stop thinking about remembering to bring my computer to work tomorrow, *ah! Rent is due in two days, I need toothpaste. Why does it smell like chicken in my apartment? Was that guy at work hitting on to me today? What was the last line of that Kesha song I liked? Maybe I shouldn't have put the broccoli in the freezer in case I want more tomorrow... LIGHT BOWL! I need to sleep and I need to quiet my mind, so I'm throwing all this junk into my box until tomorrow morning.* I say, "Light bowl, can you please hold these thoughts until I need them again tomorrow? And can you get rid of all the unnecessary ones?"

My light bowl says, "Yes!" like the backpack in Dora The Explorer, and opens its lid as all my running thoughts get pulled safely and gently into my light bowl. Done.

This tool is also very helpful when I am processing my past. After working through memories, experiencing flashbacks, feeling the emotions that come with working through abuse, it can be really difficult to close the floodgate of emotions. That is where my Save For Later Box comes in. Every time I have a therapy session, before I leave the office, I imagine placing all of the memories, feelings, and thoughts that I experienced during the session into my light bowl. Then, I take a deep breath in and exhale. I know that all of those things are safely contained in my light bowl until the next time I want to continue to work through them. I can continue with my day and not feel overwhelmed by everything I just processed.

I encourage you to use this tool each time you decide to stop reading for the day. Once you've finished an activity in this book or have finished reading for the day, close the book and imagine that all of the thoughts, memories, emotions you experienced while reading are going into your box. You are not avoiding or suppressing any thoughts, you are simply deciding that you have done enough work for the day and you are putting those thoughts on hold until the next time you're ready for them. You can also place thoughts or memories into your box while you're reading. If something pops up and you would rather not process it at the moment, put it in your box, and continue on.

So, let's create your Save For Later Box. Curl up in your Me Space and close your eyes. Imagine a box. It can be any kind of box. It can be a giant golden suitcase with eagles carved on the sides, it can be a pirate ship in the middle of the ocean where all your thoughts shift with the waves until you are ready to get back to them, or it can be a handmade wooden box with cool rustic latches. It can have a lid or not have a lid. Your box is anything that you want it to be. There are no limitations. The only stipulation is that you like it. You can even create a literal box if you'd prefer that. Use a shoebox or basket or any container to create your box and, when you have a thought you'd like to place inside, write it down on a piece of paper and put it in your box.

Once you've designed your box, imagine placing all of your stress into your box. Then place all of your fears in it, everything that has caused you anxiety today, even that woman who cut you off in traffic. You don't have to think of every stressor. You don't even have to think of any specific fears. Just say, "I'm placing my anxiety into this box." Whatever feels easiest and best for you, do that. Watch the way the box gracefully receives all of it. Your box has no fear. Your box is never too full, it just calmly accepts what you give it. Feel the trust between you and your box. When you place a thought or emotion into your box, it holds it until you come back. Your box never leaks or forgets or tries to hurt you. You've created your box and it is strong and pure and for you.

How do you feel? When I first created my box, I felt excited. I felt relieved. All of the emotions I had been carrying were now off my shoulders and safely in my box. I had a newfound tool that will never get tired or lost. It will never break or fill up. It will just be there to cleanse my mind and hold my thoughts until I am ready to come back to them.

So now we have a Me Space to work in and a Save For Later Box to hold our progress. Now we are going to develop a few more of our selves to help us through our experiences. Stay with me now. I promise I'm not leading you to crazy town.

Meeting Your Protective, Nurturing, and Spiritual Selves

Your protective, nurturing, and spiritual selves are simply versions of yourself. Think of them as guides. Your protective self protects you and gives you courage and strength when you need it most. Your nurturing self nurtures you and will comfort and love you and pet your head when you need it most. Your spiritual self is less a version of you and more the essence of yourself in connection to the Universe. You still with me? It's a much more difficult concept to grasp than your nurturing or protective selves, but just think of your spiritual self as the peaceful feeling you get when you know that you are connected to everything, that every decision you make is the right one, and that any mistake you think you've made was actually just a way to get to where you are ultimately destined to be. So, let's meet these selves.

Meet Your *Protective* Self

Close your eyes and think of a time when you protected someone fierce-ly. It could be your sister or your best friend, an animal, a co-worker, a child, or even yourself. When I did this exercise, I thought about the day I decided to move out of my partner's house and love myself enough to recognize that the relationship was no longer working.

Once you've thought of an experience when you were a protec-tor, close your eyes and identify how you feel during that moment. Do you feel fierce? Confident? Strong? Passionate? Loving?

I saw myself the day that I signed the lease for my new apartment —the first time I ever lived alone. I was exhilarated. I had done everything by myself and knew that, from that moment on, things were going to be different. I could make it on my own.

Close your eyes and meet your protective self. She has been wanting to meet you and is so excited to connect with you. Your pro-tective self is never afraid because she knows that what is real cannot be destroyed. Your truest self is real, therefore, you can never be destroyed. Your protective self is here to be your warrior for the rest of your life. Anytime you feel afraid or overwhelmed, call upon your protective self. She is you and she will protect you. This is a tool that you've always had, but may not have known about. Know that you now have the power to connect with your protective self any time you want. There is nothing your protective self cannot conquer.

Meet Your Nurturing Self

Begin by closing your eyes and think of a moment when you comforted someone or yourself. I imagined the day I was very sick after having moved out on my own. I woke up and barely had the energy to get out of bed. I started to cry and said, "I want someone to take care of me." Then, I sat up in bed and said, in the most assertive and stern way I have ever spoken to myself, "I am going to take care of me." I got up, made myself some soup, wrapped myself in a blanket, and watched movies for the rest of the day. When I visualize my nurturing self, I see myself as a goddess in all white, surrounded by a glow of light. I am gentle and loving.

Now close your eyes and meet your nurturing self. She has been waiting to hold you and comfort you. She is always with you and will never run out of love for you. Your nurturing self was there every moment anyone has ever hurt you. She consoled you in those moments, whether you realized it or not. Whenever you are afraid or need comforting guidance, ask your nurturing self. Your nurturing self will provide the love that you didn't have in moments of pain while growing up, and she will provide the love you need now.

Are you still with me? You haven't thrown away the book that is encouraging you to create more selves? Good! Let's meet our final self!

Meet Your Spiritual Self

The process of meeting your spiritual self is a bit different, but just as powerful as the other two. Close your eyes and think of a time when you felt connected to the Universe or God, Allah, Buddha, Source Energy, or whatever you want to call it. It could be a near-death experience, a time you felt connected to a loved one who had passed, a time when everything worked out effortlessly, or a time when you knew there was a higher power watching over you.

I struggled with this one. I kept trying to force myself to see a version of myself, but it felt fragmented. I didn't feel connected the way I wanted to. Then a thought popped into my head: *Let go of trying to create an image of yourself or anyone else.* So, I closed my eyes and tried again. I listened to the words and soon saw an endless ball of light. It came from my chest and it was effortless. As I looked at it, I realized that I never had to put any effort into trying to find my spiritual self. All I had to do was want to see it and it would appear. I don't ever have to put any work into connecting with my spiritual self because my spiritual self is simply the essence of who I am. It's the part of me that existed before I was born and the part of me that will exist after I pass. Your spiritual self is your true being—the part of you that can never be taken away or destroyed by anyone or anything. It is your essence, your soul. It's you.

Throw a Party

Now it's time to have a party with your selves. Close your eyes and imagine your protective, nurturing, and spiritual selves together. Do they recognize each other? If so, see how they interact. If not, allow them to meet each other. Notice how you feel knowing that these three resources are here to protect, care for, and guide you. Imagine all three of them forming a protective circle around you. I imagined them all hugging me. Know that these are your selves and even if you didn't feel connected to them previously or didn't know that they were there, they will never leave your side ever again. Call upon your selves whenever you are feeling afraid and they will shield you with protection. Call upon your selves when you are sad or lonely and they will nurture you and surround you with love. Call upon your selves when you are confused or overwhelmed and they will guide you to inner peace and freedom.

Use Words to Empower You

I wrote this book because I believe that we should be able to talk about abuse with as much ease as we talk about anything else, while eating cake pops and sipping coffee. Part of the way I believe we can make these conversations easier is by becoming comfortable and confident in sharing our own stories. This is why I want to talk about words. I believe that the words we use when talking about our stories can either help us feel more empowered or make us feel worse. I want you to feel more empowered while sharing your story, so I'm sharing a few ways that I have learned to talk about my own story that have helped me feel more empowered.

The first is how I talk about my experiences. Instead of saying, "I was abused," try saying, "I am a survivor of trauma." When I state that I am a survivor, I feel empowered. I feel badass! I'm declaring, "I experienced pain and violation and betrayal. But I am stronger and more equipped to help others heal because of it. I am damn proud of my journey!" Stating that you are a survivor also takes the focus off only the abuse and expands the conversation to include the rest of your story.

Next, I want to talk about how I discuss the abuser. I will introduce you to my sister. I will tell you cute anecdotes about my partner. I will provide too much information about the drunken nights that I've had with my friends. But I will never speak with you about my abuser. I will never call an abuser "your abuser." To call an abuser yours or mine creates some sort of relationship between two people who have no relationship. Using words that signify ownership, like "my," "your," or, "our," in connection with an abuser gives the abuser the privilege of entering into the group of people you consider to be close enough to call yours. Try saying, "My abuser." Notice how you feel. Now say, "The abuser." I cringe even typing the words, "My abuser," because I feel as if I'm putting them on the same level as casually sharing a funny story about my friend, whereas the abuser is disconnected from me. Using the phrase "the abuser" allows you to completely disconnect from the individual. The same applies to saying, "The abuse," versus, "My abuse." Using possessive pronouns when referring to abuse puts the abuse on the same level as something you lovingly own. You would say, "My jacket that I wear every day," "My favorite flavor of ice cream," or "My car that I saved all summer to buy," but referring to abuse as yours may not feel very empowering.

Lastly, I want to talk about titles. I stopped referring to my parents as "parents" years ago. Instead, when I talk about them, I call them by their names. So, from now on, throughout this book, I will be referring to my father as Tim and my mother as Lisa. Lisa and Tim were not parents. Moms and dads love their children unconditionally and do everything they can to protect them. The same goes for uncles, aunts, grandparents, partners, cousins, siblings, etc. Referring to your parents as "Mom" or "Dad" or to a loved one as "Aunt," "Grandma," etc., is a gift that you give to people who deserve your love, trust, and respect. Anyone who violates that love, trust, and respect does not deserve the title of a family member or friend. Retracting the titles from Lisa and Tim allowed me to rebuild a love for myself that I didn't even know was missing.

Separating them from the title of "Mom" and "Dad" helps me to put the two groups into separate categories: parents and family members go into a bin with love and trust and safety. Lisa, Tim, and anyone who has betrayed my love and trust go into a separate bin. Doing this has helped me understand that I wasn't unloved by my mom and dad, but I was hurt by mentally ill people who weren't capable of expressing love in a positive way.

I also plan to have kids one day, and when I do, I don't want to cringe every time I say, "Go ask your dad,"or, "Hold Mommy's hand." I want to be able to fill those titles with love, not memories of the past. I want to redefine what it means to be a father and a mother, so that I can proudly call myself "Mom" and lovingly and comfortably refer to my partner as "Dad."

This concept doesn't just apply to parents. Anyone who leads you to believe that you can trust them and feel loved by them and then betrays those promises does not deserve the title of a family member or loved one. It may feel awkward at first, but try referring to them by their name when you talk about them. You can even change their name completely if that makes you feel more comfortable. Just know that the title of Uncle, Grandma, Aunt, Mom, Dad, partner, etc., is a title that you gift to someone, and if that gift is betrayed, you have every right to take it away.

There you have it. A well developed box of tools to use on your exciting journey of healing and growth. I definitely encourage you to use each of these tools as you continue reading and completing the exercises in the book. But even more so, each time you use one of these tools, I encourage you to remember that you created it. These are some of the most powerful tools you can use while working through abuse and no one gave them to you. You created these tools for yourself. You're a badass full of self-love! Now, let's start sharing some stories.

Stop Overwhelming Yourself With the Vastness of Your Shit

I am sitting on the floor of my closet. The doors are closed, but I can see some light coming in from a crack in the door. Tim just raped me repeatedly. A part of me knows I'm human, but it feels like that part of me left. I don't know what I am right now. I don't feel anything. I don't have the energy to feel anything. My body is just a shell—it's there, but I'm not inside it anymore.

I look down at my hands. I'm not sure if I'm living. I want to touch my arms—partly to comfort myself, partly to check if this really is my body; if I'm alive. I try to touch myself, but as soon as my hand makes contact with the skin on my arm, I flinch and pull away. I can't be touched right now. My body doesn't know the difference between my own hand and someone else's touch. I pull myself toward the closet doors and into my room.

I am six years old and I still have twelve years of abuse ahead of me.

I'm not going to pretend that what you're going through is easy to overcome. As survivors of abuse, we have experienced pain on a spiritual level—pain that occurs on a much deeper level than most people experience in their entire lives. As survivors, there are layers of fear, pain, confusion, and triggers that we have to deal with every day in addition to dealing with the normal everyday bullshit everyone else has to deal with.

No, I don't consciously think about this memory every day, but this memory exists in my soul every moment of every day, as do your experiences exist within you. These memories contribute to the way I view myself, other people, and the world around me. Sometimes that contribution is a positive one, such as when I know with every molecule of my being that I am a powerful warrior who has survived hell in this lifetime. Other times, having these memories as a part of who I am can be difficult, like when I am triggered during a jiu-jitsu class by the feeling of someone else's sweat on my body.

Now, before you start getting overwhelmed by the vastness of your shit, hear me out. **Yes, overcoming the effects of abuse isn't easy, but neither was the abuse and you survived that**. You've experienced the most difficult betrayal and pain a human can experience and you survived. Any challenge you face now is laughable in comparison. You are a warrior and, from this moment on, I expect you to view yourself accordingly.

Yes, your shit is vast. And the effect of that shit is even greater. There are days when it is difficult to even get out of bed in the morning because that vastness feels so insurmountable. But you're not going to work through something so complex and painful and vast all in one day. I didn't wake up one morning and decide to take on all eighteen years of abuse at once. Instead, I started with the basic ingredients. So that's what we're going to. We are going to start with simple things you can do every day that will culminate into life changes. Let's get started:

Talk to Yourself

I am warning you right now that I am going to suggest that you talk to yourself a lot throughout this book. Like, a lot, a lot. I never learned how to love myself. In fact, I learned the opposite. I learned to believe that I was so worthless that I questioned whether I was even human. Because that is what I learned to believe, I manifested life circumstances that reflected that belief well into my adult life. It wasn't until I learned to love myself that my life began to change. The first step in learning how to love myself was simply talking to myself. I have truly experienced that checking in with myself is one of the most powerful and simple ways to improve every element of my life.

Think about how many times you've come home at the end of a long day and wished that you had someone, anyone, to simply ask, "How was your day?" Guess what? You do! Sit down at the end of a long day and check in with yourself. Ask yourself how your day went. Heck, sometimes I'll ask myself what my favorite color is because I'm not even sure what the answer will be. We spend so much time investing energy in things and people that are outside of ourselves. Taking some time to get to know ourselves again can make a world of difference. Don't believe me? Try it. Ask yourself, "[Insert name], how was your day today?" I guarantee that a wave of relief will pour from your soul as if you've been longing to hear from you for so long, because you have.

Still don't believe me? Let's reframe things a little and think about all the times you do talk to yourself throughout the day. What is the first thing you say when you wake up in the morning? If it's "Fuck" while you're hitting the snooze button, you're not off to the best start. What is your first thought when you look in the mirror? What do you say when you make a mistake or when something goes wrong? How many times a day do you call yourself names? Listen to yourself. Hear the types of words you use most frequently. Do they hold positive or negative energy? Listen to the way your body feels. Do you feel exhausted or frustrated? Maybe you even experience actual physical pain, such as back pain or joint pain. We often hold our trauma, concerns, or suppressed emotions in our bodies and it manifests as physical pain. Listen to yourself for an entire day and notice what you hear and feel. Sadly, I am willing to bet that the answers to most of those questions aren't feel-good responses. But what is even sadder is that if I hadn't asked you to think about it, you probably wouldn't even realize how much negative energy you allow to permeate your self-talk and everyday life.

I read an article about an experiment someone did with three plants. Every day, they complimented one plant, insulted the second, and completely ignored the third. Not surprisingly, the insulted plant perished pretty quickly while the complemented plant flourished. What did surprise me was that the ignored plant actually withered much more quickly than the insulted plant. How interesting is that? Acknowledging the plant - even if through insults - was still more beneficial to the plant than completely ignoring it. Now imagine how damaging it is to completely ignore or, worse, not even recognize the insults we say to ourselves every day. How quickly is our self-worth withering because we're not only insulting ourselves but also completely ignoring the effects those insults have on our mental states and physical bodies?

Have I scared you enough with plant stories yet? My point is, if you've experienced trauma, you probably had someone or even a group of people try to convince you that you are not loveable. You need to know, with every part of your soul, that you are loveable. And the first step to doing that is by kindly talking with yourself. Nourish your beautiful plant-self with loving conversation.

Greet Yourself Every Morning

One of the things I have struggled with most after surviving trauma has been connecting with myself. I spent eighteen years attempting to leave my body and disassociate from the abusive circumstances around me, so feeling disconnected from myself became the norm. I have spent years repairing the connection between my mind and body. During this time, I realized that a commitment to connecting with myself has to start from the moment I wake up.

Every morning, as soon as the alarm goes off, I greet myself by saying, "Good morning, beautiful, perfect, sun goddess, warrior queen, mermaid," or whatever variation of that I am feeling that day. Then I ask myself, "What is your intention for today?" Sometimes it's, "I intend to relax today." Other times it's, "I intend to do one thing that scares me today," or, "I intend to have fun today." I am greeting myself in the morning. I am waking up and immediately telling myself, "Girl, I see you and I love you. Let's do this thing." I am also starting my day by listening to myself. When I ask myself what my intention is, I am listening to what I need that day. Sometimes my answer is, "Today, I intend to take it slow," because that is what I need. I am telling myself, "Self, you tell me what you need today and we will make it happen together." You will be amazed by how greeting yourself in the morning and setting an intention commences a day of self-connection and guides everything that happens for the rest of your day.

Don't Be a Shitty Friend

For as long as you live, you are your only guaranteed always-friend, so you better start building that friendship. Would you angrily call your best friend hurtful names for forgetting her keys in her apartment or taking the wrong turn on her way to work? No, you would probably just laugh at her a little and move on. Would you let your friend look in the mirror and start listing off insults? Absolutely not, because you know she is beautiful inside and out. So stop being a shitty friend to yourself.

If you make a mistake, laugh it off. When you look in the mirror, tell yourself one reason why you are beautiful on the outside and one reason why you are beautiful on the inside. You are the only person in the world who will ever truly know what you've experienced. You are also the only person in the world who will ever truly know what you want and need, so become your best friend. Listen to what you are telling yourself through thoughts, emotions, and physical sensations, then lovingly provide what you need.

Say "I Love You"

Tell yourself you love you as often as possible.

Are these methods simple? Maybe even ridiculously basic? Yes, they are. They are because they have to be. During the abuse, the most basic fundamentals of who I was were violated—so violated that I questioned my own humanity. My psyche and perception of reality were so wounded that I couldn't even tell whether I was living or dead. The effects of this violation are not something that I can look at as a big picture and come up with a blanket solution for. I have to heal starting with the most fundamental elements of my mind and body. So breaking it down Barney style and starting with the basics is essential.

Check Your
Bullshit Thoughts

I am crawling around the basement. *Where did Daddy go?* I think. The concrete floors feel hard on my knees.

I see an open door for a room in the back of the basement. I crawl over to investigate. I reach over the door frame and poke my head into the room. I see there is another smaller room in the back of this room. The floors in that room are all dirt, the walls are concrete with spiderwebs on them. It's like they stopped making the house with this room.

There's Dad! I think excitedly as I spot Tim standing in the middle of the dirt room. He's pointing to something and signaling for me to come inside the room.

It's my slide! I think as I see my toy slide sitting next to Tim in the room. *I want to slide*, I think as I begin to crawl toward him.

I get a weird feeling all of a sudden. My tummy feels twisted.

Why did Daddy put my slide in there? I think. *But Daddy's smiling, he never does that, and he's telling me it's okay to come inside.*

I crawl into the room. It's cold and I don't like how my hands and knees are dirty now because of the floors. Tim pulls me toward him. He's not letting me slide on my slide. He undoes his belt. I see his private area. He pulls my head toward the area.

At that moment, I developed the bullshit thought, "I am not safe." Abuse rewires your brain. It changes the way you see yourself, others, and the world. Part of this rewiring often results in the development of negative beliefs, or what I like to call bullshit thoughts. Bullshit thoughts are things we believe yet, interestingly enough, usually don't even realize we believe. They are things that feel true, but really aren't. We learn to believe bullshit thoughts at some point in our lives and they continue to affect the way we approach life. Most of the time, these thoughts are given to us by someone else, usually an abusive person.

For example, let's say that ever since you were a little girl, whenever you tried on a shirt, your mom made you turn around to show her your back. She told you she was checking for any "rolls" around your bra line. Every time you turned around, you could feel her scrutinizing your body. Then she would say, "Let's get a bigger size. I think that will look better." Now, as an adult, you always purchase a shirt one size bigger than you actually need. You probably don't even think about it while you're doing it. You just methodically size up every time you go shopping. You do this because you believe that you have to hide the area of your back around your bra line. That is a bullshit thought. It's bullshit because it's not true, and it's bullshit because it's affecting your life every single day in a negative way. This story is certainly not uplifting, but it doesn't involve anything that seems too damaging. But that is why negative beliefs are so dangerous. They are dangerous because they can be subtle. Without even realizing it, we can live our entire lives being controlled by these beliefs that aren't even true. Girl, you have a great back. Show it off!

Here are a few of my own bullshit thoughts:

"I am not *safe*."

Believing that I am not safe has been the deepest, most all-consuming bullshit thought in my life. This belief has convinced me that I was weak, that I could never protect myself. The belief that I could not protect myself led me to seek safety in other people such as partners or father and mother figures. But because I never healed my wounds, I always chose people with their own wounds that caused them to seek dominance over me instead of "protecting" me, which led me to believe that relationships with other people were unsafe. This belief caused me to sabotage potentially healthy relationships and reject support from truly loving friends, which caused me to feel alone.

I believed I had no safety net in life, and that surviving in the world was entirely on my shoulders, which led me to play it safe by accepting jobs that didn't pay well and weren't fulfilling. I didn't pursue my dreams because I didn't believe it was safe to. I didn't allow myself to truly love or be loved because I didn't believe it was safe to. I denied love and support from friends because I didn't believe it was safe to accept. Our bullshit thoughts don't affect just one area of our lives, they sabotage each area of our lives, like cascading dominoes.

Okay, that was a little bleak, but stick with me. I promise I'll talk about how to release bullshit thoughts.

"I am not lovable."

All of us have experienced rejection in some capacity, at some point in our lives. Whether it be from a parent, a friend, a partner, or a mentor, we have all been rejected. More often than not, that rejection causes us to wonder what about ourselves caused that rejection. That very question forms the negative belief that there is something wrong with us—that we are unlovable. This causes us to put energy into false thoughts like, "My boss likes my coworker better than me," or, "The person I have a crush on likes someone else because I lack [insert list of bullshit things we believe aren't good enough about ourselves]."

All of these thoughts spiral us into an energy-sucking hurricane of self-criticism and comparison to others. All the while, the only thing we need to do is recognize that someone wasn't able to love us the way we needed or wanted, not because of us, but because of some wound of their own. And because of their wounds, we have been hanging on to the belief that we are not good enough. It's time to release that bullshit.

"I don't know what is real."

"I had a dream last night that Dad killed all of us with the axe in the garage," I nervously tell Lisa as I make my lunch and get ready to go to school.

"Why would you have a dream like that?" asks Lisa as she nonchalantly continues to move around the kitchen.

"I don't know," I say anxiously.

I finish packing my lunch and head to school.

Later that day, I walk back to the house after school. As I walk in the door, I trip over something sitting in the doorway. I look down to see the axe from the garage. "Mom, why is the axe in the house now?" I ask, terrified.

"What are you talking about, Katie? That's always been there," she replies.

At that moment, I developed the bullshit thought that I don't know what is real. *Was she right? Had the axe always been there and I was just crazy?* I learned to believe that my thoughts and feelings weren't real. I was constantly questioning reality, wondering if what I perceived as real was, in fact, real or if what I was told was reality was the truth.

For years, I manifested that same dynamic in relationships with abusive partners, coworkers, and friends. They would do hurtful things, then manipulate me and convince me that I was crazy for feeling hurt, and I believed them.

"People being attracted to me is the only way I have power."

I am at work. I was just offered a new position that I believed would offer a significant increase in salary. However, my boss just offered an insultingly low compensation rate that I know, for a fact, is significantly lower than what he offered my male coworkers. As I walk out of his office, I think, "Maybe he's treating me like shit and totally low-balling me because he thinks I'm weak, but at least I know that I have power because I am young and beautiful and he probably wants to have sex with me but can't."

I pause. *Where did that come from?* I think.

During the abuse, I had no power over anything—not over my body, my life, or my voice. In order to mentally survive, I needed to find a way to feel that I had some sort of control - any control - in my life. So, I convinced myself that I held power in someone wanting to sexually abuse me. Believing that I was "attractive" enough that someone wanted to abuse me became my only source of perceived control, power, and even safety.

As an adult, this belief manifested into a crippling focus on physical appearance. I had to be beautiful and flawless without makeup. I had to be beautiful and flawless with makeup. I became obsessed with fitness—my body never being fit enough. I hit puberty very fast and quickly as a kid and developed stretch marks around my hips as a result. I cannot even tell you how many days - actual days - I spent miserably ruminating over my stretch marks. I believed that my stretch marks permanently ruined my ability to be safe. Because of my stretch marks, my body would always be disgusting and men would always end up hurting me or cheating on me because I was not beautiful enough, powerful enough, or in control enough to keep their love.

In relationships, this bullshit thought was paralyzing. If I even suspected that my partner found someone else attractive, I would shut down. All of my power was gone, and if all of my power was gone then I was vulnerable to abuse and pain.

I developed a paralyzing fear of aging—if I didn't have my youthful beauty, I had nothing. I had to be the MOST beautiful all the time and relentlessly compared myself to every other woman I saw. If I went out and liked another woman's outfit better than mine, my night was ruined. I wanted to cry and just go home. I had to be the most perfect, most beautiful woman in the room or else someone might want to have sex with someone other than me and then all of my power would be lost. I would have nothing. I would be vulnerable and unsafe.

"Receiving is unsafe."

When I was in fifth grade, I had to wear headgear, but only at night. The dentist specifically assured me of that while I cried in his office about never being able to be seen at school wearing head gear.

"We're going to get bikes and ice cream," Tim tells me and my sister. We are elated. *This has never happened before!* My sister and I jump up and down in glee.

"But we're only going if Katie wears her headgear the entire time," says Tim.

My heart drops. I don't understand.

"The dentist said I only have to wear it at night," I nervously state. "I don't have to wear it out in public."

"If you want bikes and ice cream tonight then you have to wear it," Tim replies.

I look at my sister.
I know she wants bikes and ice cream as badly as I do.

"Okay," I say, and I go to my room to get my headgear.

We're at the store, looking at bikes. The headgear doesn't fit correctly. The back hinge keeps slipping out and stabbing me in the gums, so now I'm bleeding. I try to hold my head up and pretend that I am not bothered by any of this. But everytime I look up, I see someone else snickering at the giant metal device strapped to my mouth and head. My sister and I pick out bikes. We get ice cream. I am relieved because I can finally take the headgear off to eat my ice cream. I go to remove the device when Tim stops me.

"No, you can't take that off," he says.

"I'm going to eat my ice cream," I say.

"Keep the headgear on," he replies.

"You're not supposed to eat with it on," I plead. "It's not made for that."

"If you want your ice cream, then you'll just have to eat it with the headgear on," Tim says.

I look at my ice cream, it's already starting to melt. As tears well in my eyes, I attempt to eat my dessert. Melted ice cream drips all over my face and clothes. The metal device is covered in cream. I'm twelve years old, but I look like an infant trying to eat her first slice of birthday cake. People are pointing and laughing. I am humiliated.

At that moment, I learned that receiving is unsafe. I learned that nothing is given to me without struggle and humiliation. I learned that if someone offers me something, there are strings of shame, pain, and embarrassment attached to that gift. As an adult, this manifested in many ways, most specifically with money. Receiving things was unsafe, which meant that wanting or receiving money was definitely wrong, so I subconsciously created situations that "protected" me from receiving money, like working three jobs and still struggling to piece together enough income to pay my bills. It wasn't until I was able to recognize the bullshit thoughts I had around receiving that I started allowing myself to receive without fear and was able to fill my life with all the abundance the Universe has to offer.

"I will be hurt if I feel *beautiful*."

I am getting ready to go to a club with my friends. My hair is done, I put some makeup on, and now I'm getting dressed. I put on a dress and heels, and look at myself in the mirror.

"If you wear this, you will look like you think you're pretty, and someone will throw acid in your face," I say to myself in the mirror.

Confidence - any type of self-worth - is an abuser's most feared quality. They will do anything to tear it away from you. As a kid, I was an unshakably vibrant kid, ceaselessly optimistic and positive. This was unbearable for Lisa and Tim, who were two extremely miserable, damaged, and abusive people. I was torn down, abused, or threatened any time I demonstrated even a shred of confidence. I was constantly told stories of women who were so vain that they had acid thrown in their faces. I was told that the same would happen to me if I kept believing that I was beautiful. I spent years dressing down outfits and hiding my body to try to keep myself safe.

"I don't know what I *want*."

I am standing in front of the ice cream aisle at the grocery store, staring at all the Ben and Jerry's options. It's been forty minutes, and my boyfriend is upset with me.

"Just choose one," he says, frustrated.

Tears well up in my eyes, "I don't know which one I want."

Asking for anything when I was growing up was considered abhorrent. I was either punished for asking, shamed and humiliated before being given what I asked for, or continuously had what I wanted dangled in front of me without ever actually receiving it. Eventually, I started asking for things I didn't want in hopes that Lisa and Tim would end up inadvertently giving me what I actually wanted. After years of doing so, I had such a complex relationship with not only stating what I wanted but even recognizing what I actually did and didn't want that making simple decisions was excruciatingly difficult for me. A decision as simple as choosing an ice cream flavor became an emotionally and mentally distressing task. I had never learned how to make decisions for myself. Instead, I learned to skew or manipulate what I wanted in order to try and get the things I needed. I truly did not understand how to make a concrete decision. Something so simple as knowing how to want something and allowing myself to have it seemed so easy for other people, but I had no idea how to do it.

"Become invisible to protect yourself."

I just got back from kindergarten and Lisa is yelling at me. I don't know why. I've been quiet, and I haven't fought with my sister at all. She grabs my arm and pulls me into the kitchen. I'm scared. I don't know what to do, so I just stand still. She keeps getting closer to me and I'm trying not to flinch or pull away because she gets angrier when I do that.

She screams again and grabs the front of my dress. She rips off the top button. I'm sad because I really liked this dress. She rips off another button and then another until all the buttons on my dress are gone.

I'm not scared anymore because I'm not there. I left. I do that when I get really scared or when my mom and dad start to hurt me. I just imagine I'm somewhere else. I leave. I don't know what happened after she ripped the buttons off my dress because I am gone.

Now I'm in my room with my sister. It's been about an hour since the button incident. Lisa comes into our room. She's smiling. "We're going to take pictures now," she says and she opens the closet. "You're going to wear your fancy dresses," she says as she pulls out the dresses we only get to wear on special occasions.

I'm confused. She doesn't talk about what she did earlier. I guess we're not supposed to talk about those things, so I don't bring it up. We put on our nice dresses, and Lisa brings us back into the kitchen. She poses us against the wall she ripped my buttons off in front of an hour earlier. She takes photos of me and my sister holding hands and smiling.

Lisa prints the photo and puts it on the bulletin board in our kitchen. Whenever I look at the picture, all I can think about is Lisa ripping all the buttons off my dress.

Sick people will find ways to inflict pain. For Lisa and Tim, they looked to punish me for any reason they could find. Punishment didn't mean being yelled at or even spanked. It meant being raped. I was going to be made to feel like an animal until all my dignity was stolen and I never dared assert myself in any way again. That's what happened daily when I was growing up. I was abused when I acted out. I was abused when I seemed too confident. I was abused because I existed. Eventually, I learned to make myself small. I tried to dim every light in my body, curl up in a ball, and make myself so small that maybe, eventually, I would vanish, and Lisa and Tim would forget that I even existed at all. If I were invisible, I could hide from the abuse forever.

This habit of becoming invisible didn't go away when I escaped the abuse, and it has weeded its way into other areas of my life, such as not standing up for myself when someone is rude to me, being afraid to ask for what I want from an employer, staying in shitty situations with shitty people for too long, and never pursuing my dreams because I feared being seen. I dimmed every area of my life to try to keep myself "safe."

I could write an entire book on my negative beliefs, and I know there are still bullshit thoughts that I haven't even recognized yet. Bullshit thoughts are crippling when unnoticed. They will convince you to dull your shine or keep you from trying something you know deep down you are capable of. They will make you feel weak or insecure or afraid. They will control every aspect of your life forever if left unchecked.

So, how do we overcome negative beliefs? Well, just like we learned this bullshit, we have to release those thoughts and re-learn the truth. The best way to start is to - can you guess it?

Listen to Yourself

Hey, I didn't say, "Talk to yourself." First, I want you to listen to yourself. The interesting thing about negative beliefs is that they never really change, regardless of the situation, which actually helps you identify them. For example, you'll be doing something really simple and casual, such as getting ready to go out with your friends, and this really harsh negative statement will suddenly hurl itself into your thoughts: *Don't wear heels or someone will throw acid in your face.* When you take a moment to think about it, that statement sounds completely crazy. But our negative beliefs are so deep-seated that, if we don't make an effort to recognize them, that thought may seem totally rational. Once you know what to look for - when that really out of place, over-the-top, mean thought pops into your head - the contrast of such intense statements in such a minor situation will be easy to identify. *Aha, you can't hide anymore bullshit thoughts!* A good way to know when a bullshit thought is creeping in is when a thought makes you stop and say, "Woah, where is this coming from?" Which leads me to the next step in overcoming negative beliefs:

Talk to Yourself

You thought you got away without having to talk to yourself! But we're going to talk to ourselves again. Now that you have identified a negative belief, think about where it comes from. Ask yourself things like, "Why am I being so hard on myself right now?" or, "What am I really afraid of?" or, "Where are these thoughts coming from?" Don't worry about not being able to find the answer. Our minds are longing to connect with us. When you take the time to speak with yourself and listen, you will get an answer. Also, be kind to yourself when you're having this conversation. You wouldn't start demanding answers from a friend, so don't do that to yourself. If you have to, remove yourself from the situation that is triggering the bullshit thought, find a space for yourself, and take a few deep breaths in and out. Say things like, "Hey, you know those statements aren't true, right? You're amazing and safe to feel as beautiful as you want to all the time. I want to figure out how we can stop these thoughts from popping up, so let's think about where they are coming from…"

Teach Yourself the Truth

You learned something that was untrue. Now it's time to unlearn that lesson and reteach yourself a new one. Replace your negative beliefs with positive statements of truth. Focus on concrete things that are occurring at that moment: "I can distinguish between what is real and what is manipulation." Tell yourself that the negative belief is incorrect. "Lisa lied and manipulated you because she was mentally unstable. It was wrong of her to confuse and scare you. You are deeply connected to your intuition and truth, you have everything you need to know what is and what is not real in your life."

Set New Standards

You attract what you accept. If you accept that your bullshit thoughts of not being good enough are true, you will attract people and circumstances that reflect that belief. If you believe that you are unloveable, you will continually attract partners who make you feel unloved. If you believe that the abuse you have experienced has permanently damaged you, you will not allow yourself to overcome those experiences because that is the standard you are setting. If you want to change your life, set higher expectations. Let's start setting new standards for yourself, for the people you allow into your life, and for your life in general.

Make a list of all the things you will no longer accept from yourself:
- "I will not accept negative self-talk when I look in the mirror."
- "I will not allow the bullshit thought that I am not good enough keep me from trying new things."
- "I will no longer struggle for money."
- "I will no longer start my day with an uncountable string of profanities followed by hitting the snooze button."

Now, write down your new expectations:
- "Every time I look in the mirror, I will state one reason I love myself."
- "I will no longer allow bullshit thoughts to run my life. Instead, I will listen to myself and identify those negative beliefs and then

learn new, positive truths to replace them with."

- "Every morning, no matter how difficult it may be, I am going to greet myself lovingly as soon as my alarm goes off.
- "I will no longer struggle for money. I give myself permission to receive all the abundance the Universe has to offer."

Write down your new standards for the people around you:

- "I expect to be respected, valued, and heard in my workplace."
- "I will not associate with people who re-traumatize me or who put me in destructive situations."

Create standards for your life. I have heard so many people talk about how the world is constantly out to get them. You know what? It is, for those people, because that is the standard they have set. If you constantly expect that something terrible is going to happen, that the world will never help you, terrible things will keep happening and the world won't help you because you attract what you accept. Set a new standard.

- "I expect good things to happen for me every day."
- "I expect clear signs from the Universe that it is listening and sending help my way."

The standards you set for yourself and the world will be the foundation for everything in your life that happens next. Check your bullshit thoughts, write new and true stories, set these new standards, hold yourself and the world accountable, and awesome things will start to happen.

Get Cozy With
Your Voids

"We all have voids. Most people try to fill these voids with other people or things. But these voids are always going to be here, so the best thing we can learn to do is get comfortable with them."
—Beverly, from work

You know those moments in movies where the lead character sits down at a bus stop next to an older woman and just happens to open up to her about her entire life? Then the older woman somehow has the best advice ever and the lead character has a sudden epiphany? That's kind of what hearing that statement was like for me, except that there was no older woman. Instead, there was Beverly, the new administrative assistant at work whom I had met ten minutes ago, and, within those ten minutes, she had unleashed an unfiltered and very graphic rant about sex with guys on Tinder followed by the profound advice above. Both of which, surprisingly, were almost equally informative.

We all have voids that have developed as a result of not receiving something we needed at some point in our lives. Perhaps we grew up in an unstable home and we've developed a "safety" void as a result. Maybe we were rejected by someone we loved so we now have an "I'm not good enough" void. These voids can create feelings of emptiness that we often instinctively attempt to fill with other people or things such as partners, father and mother figures, friends, or a bowl of ice cream. Our voids are caused by wounds that only we are capable of seeing and healing. When we look to other people and things to heal that emptiness, we will always end up manifesting unhealthy relationships and circumstances that reveal the need to heal our voids even more loudly than before.

I am in the middle of a breakup with a guy I met one week after my previous relationship ended. A part of me is pulling back toward a guy I dated two relationships ago, another part of me is flirting with the idea of going on a date with a new guy, and another part of me wants to curl back up with the guy I am currently breaking up with. Despite all the pulls, my entire being is yelling, "STOP!! Please. Stop and just breathe."

It was actually embarrassing how addicted I became to dating apps—to imagining that my husband was about to walk through the doors, to the search for love. All of these things are great in moderation, but I was full-blown consumed. I knew this wasn't me. Yes, I wanted to have a family someday, but I was never consumed by thoughts about relationships before. I knew that there was something deeper going on, but I wasn't sure what it was. Why was I so suddenly consumed by the desire for love from a partner? Voids, my friend. Voids are the answer and will be the answer to many questions throughout your life. I was looking to fill a giant gaping "love me" void.

Maybe your job makes you feel like your soul is being sucked from your body through a straw. Maybe your dad is really sick. Maybe your lifetime best friend moved away. Maybe you were told since you were a child that people with money are greedy and now you struggle to allow yourself to be financially abundant. Whatever your void is, it's here and ignoring it is only going to make it feel even more vast. So let's get to know our voids.

My Voids
The *Parents* Void

Sometimes, my heart aches for parents. I have never felt an empty pain so strong as what I experience when I am really wishing I had a parent to talk to or ask for guidance from, or to simply know exists and is somewhere out there, loving me without me even having to ask them to. I was at the grocery store recently when I overheard a conversation between a father and daughter. "You want to go get some food after this?" the dad asked. The daughter shrugged her shoulders apathetically and responded, "Yeah, sure." There are times when I would give anything for a moment like that.

The *Safety* Void

I grew up in an unstable home. Naturally, this instability created a deep longing for safety that I did not know how to fill. When I met my first boyfriend, I felt like I had someone to hold me during the chaos and shield me from all the debris that chaos was throwing around in my life. I felt loved and cared for. I felt like, finally, I didn't have to work so hard to keep myself safe because I had someone who wanted to help. However, other people cannot fill your void. They just temporarily distract you from it. That's why when that relationship ended, it felt like the pain of my void was about to eat me alive. I had spent the past five years nuzzling my head into my boyfriend's arms and hiding from my wounds as I attempted to cram him into my void. Not only was I grieving the end of my relationship, but I was also faced with the ever-growing presence of my void now that my distraction was gone. Hence why I jumped into another relationship a week after that one ended, then immediately jumped on dating sites as soon as my rebound ended. I was spiraling into an abyss of failed attempts to fill my void. Voids are real, y'all. They affect many more actions and thoughts than you even realize.

So, how do we heal our voids? We get as close to them as possible.

Snuggle Up With Your Voids

We fear voids not because of what they are, but because of how they make us feel. They make us feel the suckiest of feelings: empty, unloved, scared, hurt, vulnerable, alone, uncomfortable. But our voids don't have to be scary. They're simply metaphorical "holes" in our hearts that formed when we didn't receive something we needed during a time we needed it most - the most fundamental of which is love.

No, I can't erase the life experiences that caused my voids - I am never going to have loving birth parents - but I can heal the wounds that created my voids. I can finally stop pressuring myself to find a way to somehow make my void disappear, and I can instead heal it the right way, which is by cozying up next to it and saying, "Hey, I know you're going to be here for a while, so let's watch some movies and order Chinese food." Make your voids your best friends. Feel them, feel the discomfort they hold. Lean into that discomfort and listen to what your void is telling you.

Try this: Close your eyes and take three deep breaths in and out. Ask, "What are my voids?" The first answers that pop in your head are correct. Now imagine that your voids are your best friends. Instead of fearing them, give them each a hug. Tell them, "I am going to take care of you."

Talk to Your Voids

Here we go again with me asking you to talk to some deeper, abstract part of the self. Lolz. It works and I will never stop! You are going to spend the rest of your life with these voids, so you may as well get to know them. Choose one of your voids and say, "I want to help you. In order to do that, I need to know, where did you come from?" The first memory that pops into your head is the correct one. Thank your void for being so open and honest, and then write down the memory.

Note: This can be an overwhelming activity. You don't have to do all of your voids in one day, or even in many years. This is a process that you can take at your own pace. Don't force anything. Just listen to yourself. If you don't get any responses, your mind simply may not be ready today, and that's okay, too.

Take Care of Your Voids

Your void occured as the result of a lack of love. Now is your chance to provide your voids with the love they needed but did not receive.

Ask your void, "What do you need?"

Maybe you need to cuddle up on your couch with your favorite blankets, maybe you need to break something with a baseball bat, maybe you need to hold yourself, maybe you need to go to an improv show and laugh, maybe you need a beach vacation - well, actually I think everyone needs a beach vacation - but you get my point. Whatever you need, allow yourself to have it.

Recognize the Superpowers Your Voids Hold

We hide from our voids because, from the outside, they look scary. On the surface, they show some of our deepest wounds. But our voids actually hold some of the most powerful insights into our natural talents. Our voids have to mask themselves with our greatest wounds because the superpowers they hold require a deep level of self-love and responsibility. These superpowers will be used to fulfill your life's purpose. Your voids know that only when you have the courage to heal the wounds at their surface are you ready to step into the magic of your superpowers.

I don't have loving birth parents, but I have learned that not having loving parents is part of a higher plan that largely contributed to my motivation to write this book and fulfill my life's purpose. My void has taught me to stop thinking, "I don't have parents and it makes me sad," and instead realize that "because of the lack of love in my upbringing, I am so in tune with what love truly is, and I am passionate about spreading that love to all the people around me." Loving people deeply is one of my greatest superpowers, and I know that because my void showed me. What superpowers do your voids want to reveal to you?

Try this: Rephrase each of your voids to include a superpower it's providing you with. "I have a safety void. My safety void has taught me how to discover that true safety is within me. Now that I know how to do this, I get to use this superpower to help other people discover safety within themselves instead of looking for it in other people or things."

Become Everyone You Think You Need

I said this earlier, but it is worth repeating: When we look to other people to heal our voids, we will always end up manifesting unhealthy relationships that reveal the need to heal our voids even more loudly than before. Become everyone you think you need to heal your voids.

Become your best friend, your nurturing and caring mom and dad, your most romantic loving partner. If you find yourself longing to have a loving, nurturing conversation with a mother, wrap yourself in blankets, get cozy on your couch, and talk to yourself in the gentle manner you wish a mother would. If you want to feel seen and loved by a romantic partner, be that romantic partner. Take yourself on the most romantic date you can imagine and shower yourself with compliments about your inner and outer beauty.

I am not implying that having supportive, love-filled relationships in your life isn't essential—social connection is a health necessity for us as humans. I am simply stating that we often believe that other people are the only source of certain energies we wish we had in our lives, when, in fact, we embody these energies ourselves and can access them at any time.

Finish with this meditation: Close your eyes. Take three deep breaths in and long deep breaths out. Think of the three best moments in your life. Remember how connected you felt, how fully alive you were in those moments. How did you feel? Write them down.

My three memories:

1. **Giving the valedictorian speech at my high school graduation:** I am standing at the podium in front of all my classmates. The students voted on who they wanted to speak and they chose me. This high school is the first place I ever felt safe. It is the first place I felt safe enough to start becoming who I am and who I knew I can be. Through my hella-amazing speech, I can express the love and gratitude I have for my classmates and all of my experiences here. As I speak and laugh, I can feel the flood of love returned by everyone in the audience. This is my first public declaration of all the empowerment and confidence and love I have flowing within me, despite the hell that I grew up in. I am exhilarated.

2. **Getting my first apartment:** I just broke up with my first love. I spent the past five years clinging to what I thought was safety in order to make the relationship work. I was so afraid of what would happen if I let go. But I have officially let go. It's been really freaking scary and painful. But it's also been empowering. I am standing in the middle of my empty apartment. I have spent weeks searching and applying for apartments. Now, here I am. It's over. All of that is over. I am here now, in my new haven.

3. **Starting my own business:** I just hit the "publish" button on my computer, officially launching my business website. My story is public. The deepest parts of myself are visible to the world. I am terrified—in fact, I kind of want to throw up. *What if Lisa and Tim see that I am talking openly about the abuse? Am I safe? Is this dangerous?* I don't care. I have made myself invisible for way too long. I am stepping into my true self, into my life's purpose, into my light—and it feels freaking incredible. There's no going back now. My life is launched, and I can feel the momentum of the Universe protecting me and moving me towards everything I've ever wanted for my life.

What Message Do These Memories Hold?

Where love is absent, fear develops. That is why there is fear connected to every void. For years, my fear adamantly told me, "I am not enough." I am not enough to protect myself. I am not enough to keep myself safe or happy or stable. This belief, "I am not enough," governed so many parts of my life. I struggled to stand up for myself because I feared that I wasn't enough to protect myself if someone became angry. I didn't pursue my dreams because I was afraid that I wasn't enough to be successful. I didn't allow myself to choose partners who I truly wanted to be with because I was afraid that I wasn't good enough for them to stay.

As my three favorite memories replay in my mind, a divine question pops into my head: "What do all these memories have in common?"

I reflect, then I realize that the answer is *me*. I created every single one of my favorite memories. Not one other individual created these memories for me. I built them for myself, by myself, with pure love. As I think about that, another divine thought pops into my head: "You have always been everything you needed."

I have always been enough. I have always been and always will be everything I need. With that, my voids high five me and start to heal.

What do all your best memories have in common?

Find Your Missing Puzzle Pieces, or Don't

(You're Fine Either Way)

I am doing laundry at my boyfriend's house when we start making out. We quickly move to the bedroom, where I realize that his bed is completely bare because he's just thrown his sheets and blankets into the wash. The bare mattress doesn't bother him, so I decide to not let it bother me either. We start having sex, but almost as soon as we start, I can feel myself shutting down. I feel dirty, I feel disgusting, I feel ashamed and afraid. I want to run away and hide. We stop having sex, and I immediately leave the room. I'm shaking.

I hate that mattress, I think. I can't even bring myself to be in the same room as the mattress. I leave the room and work to calm myself down.

I was frequently abused in unclean, bare spaces, such as crawl spaces in the basement or on bare mattresses. As soon as I started to feel myself being triggered with my boyfriend, I stopped being intimate with him, left the room, and reflected on the memories I have that I knew were contributing to my being triggered by the bare mattress. Because I have these concrete memories of abuse in crawl spaces and on bare mattresses to reflect on, I was able to more easily move through the trigger. But what happens when you're triggered and you don't have a concrete memory to reflect on?

Not being able to recollect abuse is difficult because our society tells us that the only way to prove that something happened is to be able to describe the occurrence in detail. We're led to believe that if we can't describe something so graphically that other people can imagine it then it didn't happen. But there are so many reasons why survivors don't remember their experiences. In my case, I was often drugged. Also in my case, I mentally blocked out a lot of the abuse as a survival mechanism. When we experience something traumatic, our brains will often block out those memories to keep us from continually reliving them and driving ourselves crazy.

Recollecting abuse is a lot like putting together a puzzle, which, as a kid, I loved doing. But as in almost every household with family members and a vacuum cleaner, at least one piece always went missing. I would spend weeks putting this glow-in-the-dark rainbow frog puzzle together in hopes that the finished product would be shellacked and hung in my room. But as I gathered what I thought were the last couple of pieces and placed them in their fitted spots, my stomach dropped. There was a piece missing.

It has to be under the table, I thought. *No, it's totally hiding on top of the finished puzzle. That always happens!*

But after several minutes of running my hands over the completed puzzle in hopes of discovering the hidden piece, I realized that the search was hopeless and it was probably stuck in the vacuum cleaner along with my marble collection and my sister's Legos. As I looked at the empty space, that little hole looked so insignificant, but I couldn't help but tear up once I realized that without this tiny piece of painted cardboard, my puzzle didn't seem whole.

People ask me to tell them exactly what happened during the abuse. When I say, "I don't know exactly what happened," people look at me in disbelief, and I can almost hear them thinking, *Come on, how can you not remember?* But I don't. I remember pieces, fragments that hint at a full memory. I have multiple pieces of the memory, there are just one or two missing pieces locked in the vacuum cleaner. Not always having concrete memories to reflect on can make overcoming the emotions and thoughts that resulted from the abuse feel even more insurmountable and frustrating.

When you have a specific memory to reflect on, it is much easier to understand why you are feeling a certain way and then overcome those feelings. There are many examples I could use, but, right now, I'm hungry, so here is a completely unrelated topic as an example:

Give Me Back My Burger

I see a woman on the street that I recognize, but at first glance, I cannot remember where from. For some reason, the more I look at her, the angrier I become. I don't like this individual, but I don't know why. I continue to look at her and try to figure out where the hell I saw her before, until, finally, I remember that ten years ago, in junior high, she stole my hamburger while I was standing in the lunch line at school.

I now have a concrete memory that justifies the feelings I experience when I see her. I also have a concrete memory that I can reflect on and say, "Ah, yes, that is why I am feeling angry when I see her. Now I recognize that the experience is over and that I am in a position in which she can no longer hurt me the way she did when she stole my burger."

Okay, maybe not those exact words, but really, I just want to be able to say, "Now I remember! Yeah, that sucked, but I do jiu-jitsu now so I can totally take her if she tries that again." Maybe that's a bit aggressive, but the point is that because I have a concrete memory that allows me to recognize the origins of my feelings, I can now reflect on and overcome those feelings.

With fragmented memories, I see the woman, I experience anger, resentment, fear, injustice, and more, and I recognize that those feelings are tied to something but I have no memory to connect them with. I have no concrete memory to use as a way to recognize why I'm experiencing certain emotions. Therefore, I feel like I cannot overcome and let go of those feelings and feel better. Instead, I feel angry with this woman, recognizing that there is a memory that could be the key to overcoming these feelings but I cannot find the missing piece.

Okay, are you over the burger analogies? Here's a real example of one of my fragmented memories.

The Steam Room

"We're going to the steam room at grandma's house," says Tim. I'm six years old, and my stomach immediately drops. I hate the steam room. It's foggy and hot and I can't breathe when I'm in there. I'm too afraid to argue, so I don't say anything. I look at my sister and can tell she feels the same way as I do about the steam room, but she doesn't say anything either.

We get to my grandma's house, and Tim leads us both into the basement of the house where the bathroom with the steam room is located. "You each get time alone with Dad in the steam room," Tim tells us. He tells my sister to wait outside the bathroom while he and I go into the steam room. The room is big, but he makes me sit really close to him.

I don't remember what happens next. Now, I am standing outside the bathroom. It's my sister's turn, and I have to wait outside. I am naked and the basement is so cold. I wish I had a towel or my clothes. I jump around to try and warm up.

So, How Do You Remember?

Having concrete memories is great and all, but how do we remember them so that we can overcome them? The answer is, you don't. From my experience, memories seem to reveal themselves as I am ready to handle them. I believe that our subconscious stores our memories somewhere we cannot access them. But as we mature both mentally and emotionally, our subconscious will reveal memories. Your puzzle pieces may reveal themselves through dreams, or after watching a movie, or reading an article, or seeing an item of clothing or smelling an odor.

How Do You Find Your Missing Pieces?

You can't force yourself to remember something that your mind isn't ready to reveal, but you can take steps toward improving trust in yourself so that your mind feels confident in revealing information to you.

Listen to Yourself

Looking back, I am amazed by all the thoughts and dreams that my mind revealed about the abuse that I ignored for years. Listening to yourself and allowing yourself to pause and really reflect on a thought that pops into your mind, no matter how scary it may seem, tells your mind that you trust and respect yourself enough to listen. It's also surprisingly comfortable to know that you always have someone to listen to you. It may sound crazy, but years of ignoring yourself influences how willing you are to believe that someone else will listen to you. Loving yourself enough to listen to your thoughts creates the foundation of respect and courage you need to heal and share your story.

Acknowledge Your Truth

As a kid, I wrote letters to people in my diary. I never gave them to anyone, but I would write them. It would say something like, "I think that, but I'm not sure – I don't know for sure – and I don't want to make such a huge accusation if I'm wrong, but I think that maybe Tim and Lisa might do some stuff that they're not supposed to do to me. But I'm not sure, so you don't really have to worry about it. I just wanted to say it."

By writing those letters, I was attempting to allow myself to acknowledge the abuse, but I wasn't quite ready to fully accept the situation. It wasn't until I was reading a book in high school that I allowed myself to acknowledge the abuse for the first time. The main character in the book was beginning to remember that her father sexually abused her. As her and her husband made love, she imagined herself as a pig on her farm. It was such a disconnected, objectifying, and almost dirty image, but I connected with it. I understood her need to disconnect from all of her emotions and leave herself completely in order to participate in intimacy. I understood the disappointment and pain that she experienced while also experiencing nothing at all. I understood the way she, while imagining herself as an object or an animal, was able to just close her eyes and attempt to keep herself whole until the intimacy was over. I knew that she hated disengaging but that she also didn't know how else to survive while being intimate. I closed the book and started crying. I said to myself for the first time, "I've experienced sexual abuse."

Five months later, I said it out loud to someone else for the first time. Allowing myself to acknowledge the abuse to myself began the process of allowing myself to tell others, which later allowed me to start working through the abuse. Once you acknowledge your thoughts and memories, pieces will begin to connect. Thoughts and feelings that you've experienced but haven't been able to place will start to make sense.

Screw the Puzzle

So I wrote this entire chapter on discovering your puzzle pieces only to conclude it by telling you to screw the puzzle. You don't need it. I spent years putting energy into trying to remember details of the abuse because I believed that those memories would unlock some hidden keys to healing from the abuse. Yes, having memories to reflect on is extremely helpful, but they aren't required. Out of all the triggers I have experienced, I can probably count on two hands the number of concrete memories I have to tie to those triggers.

So, where does that leave me? Completely okay, that's where. I simply say, "Hey, I am feeling really anxious right now (or sad or angry or scared, etc.). This definitely feels like it's connected to something from the past, but I'm free now. I am safe now. I don't need this anxiety anymore. So I'm releasing it. I love you." Boom. Simply acknowledging that your current response to a situation is probably connected to the past, and then choosing to let it go is just as powerful as being able to reflect on a source memory. So screw the puzzle. **You are whole and complete without it.**

Lovingly **Work Through Dissociation and Triggers**

I am trying to get a workout in before I teach my next fitness class. I start with some squats, but I feel so weak.

"Okay, let's try something different," I say as I quickly set down the barbell and pick up some light dumbbells. I start doing some bicep curls, but my arms feel as if they weigh a hundred pounds.

"Why do I feel so weak?" I say, frustrated.

A thought pops into my mind, *Meditate about it.* But I don't have time for that, so I ignore it and keep trying to workout. I put the dumbbells away and decide to do some push-ups.

The thought persists, *Stop moving and just meditate.*

"Ugh! Fine," I reluctantly state. I grab a yoga mat, lay down, and close my eyes. I take a deep breath in and out.

"Why do I feel so weak when I workout?" I ask.

Immediately an image of me exercising appears in my mind. I can see my physical self doing burpees, but my soul is hovering above me. I realize that my body and mind are completely disconnected. I realize that I'm not only disconnected during workouts. In fact, I live the majority of my life physically in one place while my mind is somewhere else completely. I am exhausted almost all the time because, without a mind-body connection, it feels as if I am trying to push my car to wherever I am going instead of sitting inside and driving to my destination.

Dissociating had become an everyday habit. The scary thing was, I hadn't even realized it. The scarier thing was, I didn't know how to stop doing it.

In order to survive the abuse as a child, I dissociated. My non-doctor definition of dissociation is when you mentally shut down in certain situations. Physically, you are still there, but you have essentially left your body mentally. As a child, I dissociated constantly—so much so that I don't have very many memories. The memories that I do have are vivid because they are the few instances in which I was actually embodied. They are the only memories that I can recall in first person—viewing the world through my own eyes as opposed to feeling as if I am floating above myself and witnessing my life as if I am watching a movie. Dissociation was an effective survival tool during the abuse because it allowed me to completely separate myself from the abuse. I mentally left my body so that I could disconnect from the reality I was living in and protect myself from emotionally breaking.

Dissociation became my norm. Soon, I was living outside my body far more than I lived within it. Instinctively, I dissociated at any sign of discomfort or danger. Although this was an effective tool as a child, as an adult, away from the abuse, leaving my body the second I feel any type of discomfort prevents me from living a healthy life; it prevents me from experiencing uncomfortable emotions required to heal wounds, it keeps me from being present during beautiful life experiences, it inhibits me from connecting with people I love, and it disallows me from being deeply in tune with myself.

As I started openly speaking about dissociation with other women, I realized that trauma is not the only experience that causes us, as women, to disconnect from our bodies. Like many women, I hit puberty hard and fast. It felt like I went from a girl to a fully developed woman overnight. My body completely changed into something I didn't recognize or know how to move. *How do I even run with these boobs?* I thought. While I grew increasingly unfamiliar with my own body, boys in my class, as well as adult men, started noticing my body and looking at me in ways that made me even more uncomfortable. That, in addition to the abuse I was already experiencing, made me feel as if my body was the most unsafe place to be in the world, so I left it. Of course, I was still living in my body, but my mind-body connection was completely lost. Whether women have experienced abuse or not, I do believe that disconnecting from our bodies at some point in our lives is an experience most women are familiar with. As a result, many of us struggle with dissociation.

Know the Signs

Start by figuring out how to identify when you are starting to dissociate. Once you know what to look for, it is much easier to stop the process before it escalates. Pay attention to your patterns. What happens when you dissociate. How do you feel or not feel? What happens in your mind or around you?

One feeling that is a sure-fire sign that I am dissociating is exhaustion. I cannot tell you how many times I wake up in the morning, have breakfast, maybe even have some tea, and read my book, then head out to work. While I am driving to work, my eyes feel heavy and, without thinking, I blurt out, "Wow, I am exhausted. How am I exhausted? I haven't even started my workday yet." I spent the entire morning completely outside my body. Yes, I physically got up, made breakfast, drank some tea, read, and headed to work. But mentally, I was somewhere else the entire time. In fact, my mind was in twelve different places at once, thinking about to-do lists, bills, grocery lists, work, friends, relationships, that show on Netflix I want to try watching. Additionally, there are times when I am working out or instructing a class and it feels as if it is taking every ounce of energy I have just to move my body. That exhaustion is a clear indicator that I have mentally left my body and am just trying to press forward with my physical self.

Another sign that I am beginning to dissociate is what I will call "the haze." The haze usually occurs when I am dissociating as a result of being triggered (something we'll talk about in a minute). Something will happen that will remind me of a situation from my past and I will feel myself mentally shutting down. I don't hear what people are saying to me, everything seems to move in movie slow motion, and a haze seems to descend over everything in front of me—it's like this weird wall of haze forms that completely cuts off everyone around me.

When my mind and body are connected, I feel strong and connected and safe within myself. I experience the essence of myself and I recognize that nothing in the material world matters—none of the stresses or fears that I was previously consumed by are significant. I simply exist with myself and recognize that this alignment is all that matters. Maybe it sounds a bit hippy-like, but truly being embodied and fully connected with yourself changes your perspective and reminds you of how completely safe and powerful you are. It wasn't until I learned to recognize that I was beginning to dissociate that I was able to develop methods to help me stop. Take some time to learn your signs.

Breathe

Take time to breathe. Listen to the environment around you. Allow yourself to feel yourself reconnecting your mind and body. Feel the power and peacefulness that comes with that connection. Take deep breaths in and long exhales out.

Be Patient

Maybe this doesn't work the first time you do it. Maybe your mind isn't ready to come back yet. That's okay. Don't panic and don't get frustrated with yourself. Just keep checking in with yourself.

Meditate

I cannot emphasize enough how powerful meditation is for connecting with yourself. I am not naturally a calm, patient person. For most of my life, I was go, go, go, and then go more until I either passed out or got sick enough that I was forced to stop. So meditating can be difficult for me. And when I say meditate, I am not telling you that you have to light candles, set up a meditation nook, and sit with your legs crossed while chanting mantras (although that is an awesome idea, too). You can meditate anywhere, anytime - maybe not while driving or operating heavy machinery.

Some people love guided meditations. I don't love the formality of guided meditation so, for me, meditating is laying on my couch or the floor of my apartment, taking three deep breaths in and long exhales out, and then imagining that I am sitting on a stone that starts at the top of my head and floats all the way down until I gently hit the bottom of my core. I'm in the root of my body. Once I'm there, I simply ask myself, "Self, what message do you have for me?" This simple question has led to many powerful realizations. Even setting a timer for just three minutes and committing to meditating for those three minutes every day can make a huge difference.

Find a Physical Activity That Requires All Your Attention

Jiu-jitsu was one of the first physical activities that I tried and realized that an entire hour had passed and I stayed embodied the entire time. At all times, I am recognizing where someone is around my body and finding ways to leverage their body to get myself into a better position. There wasn't a second available for me to lose focus or else I would be pinned. I know some people who love to race cars because they can't pause to think about what they have to do at work tomorrow or they will crash. I am never suggesting that you put yourself in dangerous situations, but find an activity that requires all of your attention, an activity that does not allow you to zone out, even for a second.

Dissociation does not only affect our connection with our bodies - because we disconnect from our bodies when we dissociate - it can also result in a lack of connection with our sense of identity. I don't know what I look like. I know that sounds crazy, but, most of the time, I really am not sure what I look like. When I first started high school, people would walk past me, wave, and say, "Hi, Katie." I was confused by this. I thought, *How do they know who I am? What are they recognizing?*

Because I have spent so many years completely disconnected from myself, my own identity seems elusive to me. Allowing myself to not only see myself but also allow the world to see me has been one of the most significant journeys in stepping into my self-love and happiness. So how can we help ourselves become beautifully and fully visible?

Take Some Selfies

That's right, I said it! This may seem like one of my most ridiculous suggestions, but hear me out. Although we often like to condemn selfie-takers as narcissistic or make fun of them for their preoccupation with taking photos of themselves, selfie-takers are practicing one of the most important things we're supposed to learn to do from the time we're babies: self-identify.

When you think about, we rarely see ourselves. For most of the day, we don't see ourselves at all until we cross a mirror (or storefront window). I spent my life not knowing what I looked like, so my entire perception of my appearance is based on other people's reactions to and statements about me. I never allowed myself the opportunity to see me and to know, for myself, who I am. When I take a selfie, I am looking at myself. Taking photos allows me to take back my identity and allow myself to be seen on my own terms. Selfies are beautiful, y'all!

Draw Yourself

One of the most powerful experiences I had was when I randomly decided to draw myself in my mid-twenties. I was bored at work and doodling when I started to draw myself. "Here is my flowy mermaid hair," I said as I drew curls. "And my adorable nose and structured cheek and jawbones. I really like those," I continued. "Ah, the eyes I'm drawing don't really match. My eyes are much kinder in real life." As I finished, I realized that was one of the first times I ever recognized myself. Not only that, but I recognized myself lovingly, taking the time to really capture everything I loved about myself. Try it! Take ten minutes to draw yourself. While you're drawing, really notice all the things you love about yourself.

Look in the Mirror and *Talk* to Yourself

How many times do you see yourself talk during the day? Almost never. It was amazing to see the facial expressions and subtle mouth movements that I never knew were part of who I am until I watched myself talking in the mirror. Set a timer for five minutes and spend that time talking to yourself in the mirror. I know, it's an even weirder version of my normal suggestion of talking to yourself. Just try it!

Allow Yourself to Be *Seen*

I developed the bullshit thought that if I feel beautiful, I will be hurt. But honestly, the thought of everyone who sees me being filled with rage at the fact that I feel good about myself is actually pretty freaking self-involved. It's totally understandable that I developed that bullshit thought, because that is exactly what happened when I was a kid who demonstrated any confidence in a house where it was necessary for me to feel like dirt in order for the abusers to stay in control. But now that I am away from the abuse and living my life as an adult, it is insane for me to think that everyone around me could give a shit about what I am doing or how I look.

Think about it. How many people do you really pay attention to throughout the day? Not many. You are safe to shine now. Additionally, You are capable of deciphering between wanted and unwanted attention. As a kid living in an abusive household, all attention was bad attention. But that isn't the case anymore. The cool part is that, after years of experiencing bad attention, I can identify it from five-hundred miles away. I know when someone's gaze does not have good intentions, and I have the power now to stay away from it or to seek help when I need it. Wear that dress you always worry is too over-the-top, pitch your idea at the next meeting, tell that joke to your new group of friends.

The past is just that, the past. Now it's time for you to connect with yourself, learn who you truly are, and let yourself shine.

Dealing With Triggers

I cannot talk about dissociation without also talking about triggers because being triggered is one of the most common causes of dissociation. My non-doctor definition of a trigger is any image, sensation, sound, smell, or experience that reminds us of the trauma we've survived. The thing about triggers is that they can feel just as real as the trauma. There are times when I am so triggered that I cannot separate the past from the present moment—it feels as if I am reliving the trauma all over again.

I am carrying the last few boxes into my new apartment when I notice the vents in the wall. They are almost identical to the vents where cameras were hidden in the house I grew up in.

There's a camera in there, I think as I look up at the vent at the top of my bedroom wall. But I ignore the thought and continue unpacking. Hours pass, and I continue organizing my things, but I can't stop looking at these freaking vents.

There's one over there, I notice. *Oh, and another one there*, I think.

In my living room alone, there are four vents. I can feel that I'm being watched, my every move being scrutinized and abusively gazed at.

By the time I finish unpacking, I am sweaty and covered in moving dirt. I decide to shower. As I walk into my bathroom, I notice another vent. I try to ignore the fear that is pushing its way up from the bottom of my stomach. I start undressing, but I can feel them watching me. I don't want to undress anymore, but I have to shower. I feel dirty and disgusting.

I'll never be alone, I think, panicked. My body shifts. Just as I did as a kid, I change the way I move and hold myself in an attempt to hide my body and shield my movements from the camera.

I am being violated. Privacy doesn't exist. Someone is doing something bad to me and I can't do anything to prove it or stop it. A floodgate of emotions bursts open and soaks me.

I run out of my bathroom and into my bedroom, but there are vents there, too. I run into my living room and am immediately caught by each vent there.

"Breathe," I attempt to say to myself, but I can't. I can't catch a full breath. I'm hyperventilating.

"You are being triggered. This isn't real," I try to tell myself, but those thoughts are quickly flooded by fear and panic.

The only space in my entire apartment without a vent is a small hallway connecting my bathroom to my bedroom. I run to the hallway and curl up in a ball on the floor and hold myself as tightly as I can, hoping I'll vanish and they won't be able to see me anymore. I am crying.

I try to move, but I can't. I am frozen.

I continually repeat, "I don't know what is real," as I weep.

Rationally, I knew there weren't cameras in my apartment, but I could not convince myself of it. Every feeling of violation, never being alone, being watched, fear, disgust, and pain that I experienced growing up felt just as real at that moment as they did ten years before. I truly felt as if I could not distinguish between what was real and what was just in my head. At that moment, in my mind, there WERE cameras in my apartment. That is a trigger.

We can be triggered by anything at any moment, which sounds scary, and it can be. But when we know how to identify a trigger, we can move through the experience and heal the memory much more smoothly.

Listen for Your Voice

Although it was almost completely drowned out by the fearful voices of years of past selves, the voice of my true self was still with me through the entire trigger. Through every thought that convinced me to panic, my true voice calmly reassured me, "You are being triggered. This is just a trigger." Your true self is who you truly are. Essentially, your true self is your soul. It's the part of you who can never be destroyed and was never damaged or even scratched by the trauma you experienced. This part of you - your true self and voice - never leaves you. Yes, it may be difficult to hear among the panicked thoughts and emotions of a trigger, but it's there. And this voice will guide you out of this trigger.

Focus on this voice. You can find it by listening for the calm within the storm. Your thoughts may be racing, your emotions running wild with adrenaline and fear, but your true voice will remain calm and consistent. Listen for this consistency.

"You are being triggered," my true voice calmly states, "You know what is real. "Go outside," it calmly advises.

Leave the Situation

Do not stay in a place that is triggering you. I used to think that I needed to push myself to stay in a situation in order to overcome a trigger—that doing so made me stronger in some way. The opposite is true. The most courageous thing you can do while being triggered is to love yourself. So leave the situation. I could not stand to be in my apartment any longer, so I ran outside.

Get Back to the *Present* Moment

Triggers pull you back into the past. Just like we couldn't heal our wounds while we were experiencing them, we cannot move through a trigger when we are reliving our pasts through that trigger. To move through them, we have to get back to the present moment, which, when you are panicked, is not always an easy process. So start as simply as possible by stating facts of the present moment. "I am outside of my apartment. I am in Pittsburgh. I see my car and it's blue. I see a yellow bus. I am standing in the parking lot. My neighbor, Barb, is walking down the street." Stating facts that are occurring now can help your mind stop racing through past memories and bring you back to the present moment. If forming entire sentences is too much in the moment, just list colors you see. "Yellow, blue, green."

Breathe

These statements will help you begin to move back to the present and create enough calm to begin focusing on your breath. Continue stating your facts while you take deep breaths in and long exhales out. "I am here." Breath in and out. "I am in the present." Breath in and out. "The abuse is over and I am in the present moment now." Breathe. "I am next to the tree in front of my apartment building."

Do Whatever You Need to Feel *Safe*

This is ESSENTIAL. You wouldn't tell a scared little kid to shut up and go back to bed if she were having nightmares, so don't tell the scared little girl part of yourself to shut up and deal with your fear. Instead, listen to what you need at that moment, and then do it. Sometimes, you need to call your friend and ask them to come over. Sometimes you need to turn on all the lights in your house for the third time that night to make sure no one is in the house. Sometimes you need to curl up on your couch and wrap yourself in heavy blankets. Sometimes you need to take a screwdriver and remove all the vents in your apartment to check that there aren't any cameras. Do it. Turn on the lights, hold the hand of your little girl self, and check the closet for monsters with her. When you feel calm enough, ask yourself, "What do I need to feel safe right now?" Then do it, without hesitation.

Not all triggers will be as significant as this one. There are days when I experience a small trigger, like hearing a song on the radio that reminds me of abuse I experienced in junior high. During that moment, moving through the trigger may be as simple as turning off the song.

There may also be moments when you aren't able to immediately reflect on a smaller trigger. If you are in the middle of the gym locker room or getting ready to present in front of your entire team at work or if you just need to watch a movie and relax for the night, you may need to put the healing process on hold temporarily.

Put It in Your Light Box

I encourage you to always, at the very least, take the time to make yourself feel safe again after experiencing a trigger, whether that be by connecting with your nurturing self or returning to your Me Space or using the techniques above to get back to the present moment. That said, if you aren't in the headspace to process the trigger and work through it, that's okay. Believe me, I get it. There are moments when I simply need to move through the trigger and feel safe again without putting the energy into identifying the memory it comes from and healing the wounds associated with that memory. Thank your body for keeping you safe and then place the memory, the feelings, the triggers into your light box. You are not avoiding the memory, you are simply placing it in your light box temporarily, from which you can retrieve it later.

What If All of That Doesn't Work?

Triggers can stick with us for some time. When I was triggered by the vents in my apartment, I spent days feeling dissociated. I knew I dissociated, but no matter how hard I tried, I couldn't convince myself to come back. It was as if my mind was a toddler who I had accidentally scared away and didn't know how to convince her that it was safe to return.

For the next week, I could feel that I was disembodied. Yes, physically, I was going to work and talking with friends and living my life but, mentally, I was completely disconnected. I stopped going to yoga, I stopped eating foods that were nourishing and healthy, I stopped working out. I was ignoring the fact that my mind-body connection was gone. I was ignoring it because it scared me. I wanted to feel grounded and connected again, but nothing seemed to work. Finally, I closed my eyes and simply breathed. I was able to quiet my mind enough to meditate for a few minutes. I imagined myself on a pier at sunset. I was standing on the pier when myself appeared with me. It felt like the presence of my best friend had finally returned. "Hey! You're back" I said. "I am really happy that you're back." All the anxiety I had been experiencing the week prior suddenly felt so insignificant. I felt comforted, strong, and safe again. That is the difference between dissociation and being embodied. So, how do you come back to yourself?

Choose a Meeting Spot

You know when you go to a busy theme park with your family and before heading towards the rides your mom says, "This giant apple ride is going to be our meeting spot. If you get lost, just get back to this spot and I will come find you again." Develop a similar meeting spot with yourself. "Self, when you feel like you need to run away and disconnect from me, let's meet on this pier at sunset. It'll just be me and you and we can relax."

Talk to Yourself

Imagine that you're at your meeting spot, even if another part of yourself hasn't shown up yet. Talk to yourself. Ask, "What was it that scared you away?" Then ask, "What can I do next time to help you feel safe?"

Thank Yourself

At their worst, triggers are terrifying and confusing. At their best, they are inconvenient and scary. So, either way, they suck. But they are also a testament to how awesome your body is. Your body is remembering something that you may not be able to recall consciously and reminding you to stay clear of things that hurt you in the past in order to keep you safe now. The takeaway from that is, your body freaking LOVES you! Your body is telling you, "I love you so much that I have memorized every detail of this terrible moment you experienced so that I can spend the rest of your life reminding you to never get anywhere near any of these things again." Yeah, it sucks when you're trying to comfortably hold hands with your partner, but these triggers, in a way, are some of the most beautiful testaments to how dedicated your body is to loving you and keeping you safe.

I understand that these triggers can be frustrating, but you have experienced enough hurt, so don't beat yourself up. Instead –

High-Five Yourself
You deserve it.

Know, Without a Doubt, That *Safety* Is Within You

I am laying on the floor of the living room. Tim is hovering over me. He's holding me down, and I can feel him touching me. I don't want him to touch me. I really, really don't want him to touch me.

Usually, I go away when he touches me. My body is still there, but I go somewhere else in my mind. But my mind won't go away this time. I'm still here, and I can feel him touching me, and I hate it.

I begin to panic. I scream. I see Lisa in the next room.

"Mom!" I scream. "Help me!"

She looks up at me. I thought she would look horrified and come running over to save me. But she just looks at me. She doesn't move. She doesn't look concerned at all. I'm scared.

"Please!" I shriek, as I start weeping. "Mommy, please make this stop!" I scream louder and cry harder. I look at her, and she looks at me. Tim holds me down, and I realize that Lisa is not going to help me.

As a child, I wasn't able to physically protect myself from two adult predators. As a result, I developed the bullshit belief that I couldn't protect myself, that I am not safe. So, I started looking for safety in external places and people outside of myself. I looked for safety in boyfriends, in a teacher or coach who was like a father or mother figure, in kettle-corn while curled up on the sofa watching a movie with my friends, in treating myself to something at the store when I was feeling sad or happy or anxious or excited, in imagining the apartment I lived in with friends during college. I would also look for safety in perfection. I would agonize about my pillows being in the perfect position, my blanket being folded exactly the way I like, my candles being lit and my twinkle lights being positioned a certain way - all so that my apartment could be perfect, and then, maybe, I could finally feel safe.

If I had a movie night at my apartment, I would neurotically contemplate which movie to watch. I wasn't just choosing a movie, I was choosing the perfect movie. I was choosing a movie that would elicit positive feelings so as to protect me from feeling unsafe. I was choosing the perfect movie to perfectly complement the perfectly placed pillows on the perfectly made bed for my perfectly executed movie night. *Whew!* I feel exhausted just thinking about all that pressure. Everything had to be perfect because, in my mind, that perfection was what was finally going to make me feel safe. I stood in front of the Redbox kiosk, close to tears for what seemed like an eternity, because if I chose the wrong movie, the whole night could be ruined and I wouldn't feel safe.

I put the same pressure on my partner. If I was feeling vulnerable, or I was stressed out at work, or I was nervous about an upcoming performance, I wanted him to hold me until I felt safe. But it never worked. After a while, I resented him for not "saving" me from the bad feelings, and he resented me for pressuring him to do so. My point is, all the cuddling and movie nights in the world will never replace bad feelings with safety. It took me years to realize how desperately I had looked for safety in other places, and it took even longer for me to realize that nothing and no one can give me safety. Safety is within me. Now, this is definitely easier said than believed and lived. But it's true, and I am going to help you discover it for yourself.

My partner and I had been together for over five years when we broke up. For a long time, I would say to myself, "It's just a break-up, get over it." And it was just a break-up, and I needed to move on. But break-ups suck. They really do, and this one really sucked for me. He was the first individual I ever dated. He was the first man I was ever able to be intimate with. He was the first man I ever felt safe with, loved by, and who I loved back. His family felt like my family. We lived together and our home was one of the first real homes I ever had. I believed in and deeply wanted our relationship to be proof that I could be loved unconditionally—that it was possible for me.

The day after we broke up, I got up, went to work, got in my car to drive home after work and had a full-blown meltdown. I cried uncontrollably, like that gif of Kim Kardashian's ugly cry times ten, plus full-scale snot bubbles. I continued to cry in my car for about five hours. I couldn't drive home. I could barely speak. I felt like I had been thrown naked into the middle of the ocean. I felt vulnerable, I felt terrified, I felt confused and unsure. I was making plans to find an apartment, to leave a family I loved. I was about to walk away from so many things that finally helped me feel safe.

There's a lot more about that, but let's fast forward to about a month later.

I moved out. I am in my own apartment, and I just signed up for a trial period of yoga classes - thank the Universe for discounted classes on Groupon. I always arrive about fifteen minutes before class starts so I can meditate. On this day, I feel especially sad about not having my ex-boy-friend in my life anymore. I can't stop thinking about him, and I feel like I just want to curl up in a ball and cry. I take a breath and say, "Woah, I understand feeling sad about a break-up, but there is way more to this sadness." So, I talk to my heart, "Heart, why am I so sad?"

I immediately see my six-year-old self, curled up and weeping in the basement crawl space, where I was frequently abused as a child. I realize that, although I had known for over a year before the breakup that my ex and I were not a good fit, my little girl self clung to the safety I felt through him. Now, he was gone, and my six-year-old self was terrified and locked back in that scary, dark, empty room alone. I immediately kneel down and hold her. I say, "Baby, it's okay. I promise, I am here, and I am never going to leave. I love you so much and you are safe." I hold her as tightly as I can. I rock her and tell her how much I love her, how everything is going to be okay, how I am going to be here with her forever, how I am never leaving.

Suddenly, my six-year-old self and I are standing in the park. She smiles and starts laughing as she runs to the sandbox to play. I can see that she is released from the years of fear that she had been trapped in. I loved her the way she needed to be loved, and now she has let go of the dark, terrifying room she was confined in. I have let go of that dark, terrifying room. Now, she's at the playground where she plays and laughs safely.

At that moment, I realized how desperately I looked to my ex-partner to make me feel safe, to give me safety. I also realized that relationships were not the only spaces I looked to for safety. I had been holding on to people, things, and places for years in an attempt to feel safe. Most significantly, I realized that I have the power to hold my six-year-old self and help her feel safe again. No one else has that power. Safety is in me. No one and nothing else can give it to me. Safety is in you, too.

Where Are You Trying to Find Safety?

Do you look for safety in a partner? In the puppy section of Petland? In a stack of warm cupcake-flavored pancakes with rainbow sprinkles? In the house you grew up in as a kid? Write down where you find yourself looking for safety.

Think About How You Feel

Write down the feelings you associate with each of these things. For example, if you find yourself seeking safety in food, write down how you feel when you eat: comforted, nostalgic, peaceful, happy, rewarded, relaxed, etc. Now, close your eyes and really feel those emotions you listed. Understand that you are allowing yourself to experience these emotions, not the puppy or stack of warm pancakes. Acknowledge that you are capable of experiencing these emotions at any time because you are the one who is creating them, nothing and no one else.

This is When I Tell You to Talk to Yourself Again

Think back to the last time you cried. Why were you crying? How did you feel? Where were you? Who were you with, or were you alone? Think about what you needed in that moment. Maybe it was a hug, maybe it was advice, maybe you just needed someone to tell you that you're doing a really great job with this whole living life thing. What if you could go back and give your past self what you needed at that moment?

Well, you can, and it's amazing. Talking to my past selves has been one of the most significant and comforting things I've ever experienced. It's a chance for you to arrive at the moment when you needed love most and to give yourself exactly that—all of your love, all your compassion, all your hugs, and metaphorical stacks of warm pancakes with rainbow sprinkles—all of your safety.

So, let's do that. Let's go back and make your past selves safe again.

Find and *Save* Your Past Selves

I am in high school, and the rage is too much for me to handle. It's late at night, and I know that if I go to sleep, I am going to be abused. I know that my parents are doing terrible things to me, but I don't know how to prove it and I don't even know how to tell someone about it.

"Fuck!" I scream. I am so deeply hurt and scared, but I can't even begin to process that pain, so I stick with anger. I grab a baseball bat and run to my front yard. Fighting back tears, I start bashing in the grass with the bat. Lisa opens the front door.

"Katie, come back inside," she says in an eerily calm manner. "The neighbors are going to see you." There is no concern behind her words. She's not scared or worried. In fact, she almost seems entertained by my actions.

I think my soul is broken. I barely have the energy to feel anything anymore. I don't understand how Lisa can stand there so calmly when she knows that her abuse is the reason I feel as if I'm going crazy. I take my bat, slowly walk back inside, and go to bed.

I cannot tell you how many times I have remembered that time and thought, "I wish I could go back and save me."

Guess what? I can! You can, too! It's called past self work.

Past self work is some of the most powerful healing work you can do. Through this work, you get to go back in time and provide your past self with what you needed at that moment but didn't receive. I can go back and allow my past self to tell me about the abuse she doesn't understand. I can listen to her and validate her feelings. Then I can take her to a safe place, away from the abuse.

Some people are intimidated by past self work because they think it means reliving painful moments from the past. But I like to think of past self work like the work of a firefighter. A firefighter voluntarily dives into the flames of a burning building, but while there, she doesn't try to grab furniture or save the television. She doesn't let the smoke from the fire cloud her focus. She is there for one reason and one reason only: to save those who are stuck in the building and need to be saved. We are doing the same thing for our past selves. When we go back for our past selves, we will be moving through some of the scariest, most heated times in our lives. But we're not going back to relive those moments or to allow those moments to engulf us and affect us all over again. We are there for one sole purpose: to save our past selves. Your mission is to remove your past selves from those memories, and they are waiting for you, so let's get started.

Figure Out Who Needs Your Help

So many of my thoughts, feelings, reactions to situations, and fears are all somehow tied to experiences of the past, and my past selves are a huge part of that. So now, when I feel difficult emotions, I recognize that those feelings may be stemming from one of my past selves. So I ask, "Who is feeling this way?" It's pretty amazing how quickly an image of one of my past selves pops up in response.

Comfort Your Past Self

Just like you need to get things off your chest sometimes, so do your past selves. Ask them, "Tell me how you are feeling. What's going on?" One of my past selves told me that she felt like Pac-Man, just bouncing off the walls, trying to find direction and not get eaten by those ghost things. I told her that I understood that trying to figure out how to live life without a homebase and without parents is really scary and lonely. She started crying and told me how lonely she was feeling. Ask your past self if you can hold her. Maybe she wants a hug, maybe she wants you to pet her head, or rub her back, or go for a walk with her. Ask her what she needs to feel safe now.

Ask Your Past Self Where They Want To Go

One of my past selves was stuck in a time when I had just graduated college and many of my friends had moved away. I felt alone and scared. I asked my past self, "Where do you want to go?" Excitedly, she said "To the dining hall." The dining hall was where I had dinner with all of my friends every night during college. It was where I felt safe, connected, and loved by the people around me. In an instant, we were there. She walked into the dining hall and every one of her friends were there, excitedly waiting for her to join them. She burst into laughter as she talked about all the shenanigans they were going to get into once they went out after dinner. I could feel how truly loved my past self felt for the first time in years. She needed this. I needed this. As I watched her fill with joy, I felt lighter. I knew that the scared little girl from a few years ago was safe and happy now. I was safe and happy now.

Release Your Past Self

This is the best part because you get to let go, knowing that that part of yourself is healed. Spend a moment watching your past self beam with happiness, then, as she looks at you, she will smile and wave, and you can smile and wave back, knowing that she is safe now. Take a deep breath in and out, and come back to the present.

Now It's Your Turn

For me, that day at the yoga studio, it was my six-year old self who was being abused by both parents every day. A few months later, it was my recently graduated self who missed her friends and school. For you, it could be your past self from last week or ten years ago. Arrive in the moment and hold yourself. Listen, then tell yourself what you need to hear in that moment. Hold yourself in the way that you need to be held. Be the person you need.

What happens next is magic. Your past self will feel lighter. She will trust you, feel loved by you, feel safe. Ask your past self, "Where do you want to go?" One of my past selves wanted to jump into a giant pool of gumballs, another wanted to float on a cloud with light-filled angels protecting her and petting her head, staying with her while she slept, another wanted to be in a swimming pool with palm trees with an ice cream cone that never melts. Ask your past self where she wants to go and then go there with her.

Watch as your past self laughs and dances and enjoys and swims and is lighthearted for the first time ever. Watch as the fear and sadness of the moment you met her melt away and feel peace knowing that the fear and sadness are gone. Hold your past self one last time and tell her that this is where she gets to stay forever, and if there is ever another place she wants to go, she can go there, too. Tell her that she will never have to go back to the place she was—the place of fear and sadness. Hold her tightly and feel your love pouring into her. Notice how the love you're giving your past self comforts your current adult self as well.

One time, as I was holding my past self and getting ready to say goodbye, I said "You are okay," and she held my face, looked into my eyes, and said, "You are okay, too." That is the incredible thing about this exercise - the benefits are cyclical and endless. We are able to comfort parts of ourselves that felt helpless and left behind in the past. In doing so, that part of ourselves is healed and we can feel more at peace in our adult selves. Sometimes, our past selves even comfort our current selves.

Okay, are you still with me? Because I just told you about the time I talked to my six-year-old self in a pool of rainbow gumballs. But you're reading this book for the same reason that I am writing it - because you know that there are parts of you that need to heal, and you know that you are the only one who can do that healing, and you want to know where to start. So stop being all "Is this woman on drugs?" and just try it. You have nothing to lose. You do, however, have a six-year-old self waiting for you to help her feel safe.

Redefine *Touch*

> *"At the end of the day, people won't remember what you said or did,*
> *but they will remember how you made them feel."*
> *-Maya Angelou*

I am standing in the shower and I am crying because I am so freaking frustrated. All I have to do is lather the soap on my body, rinse it off, and I'll be done with the shower. But I can't. I can't put the soap on my body because I can't touch myself.

"This is my hand," I say. "It's just my hand," I plead. But it doesn't matter. The feeling of touch on my body is unbearable, so I stand in the shower feeling helpless.

There are times when I can't wipe after peeing because simply touching my vagina makes me feel violated. Memories are stored at the cellular level, so, in other words, memories are stored in our bodies. I may not remember what was said or what exactly happened during the abuse, but my body remembers exactly how the abuse made me feel. My body stored that memory deep in its cells so that, now, sometimes just the touch of my own hand on my body can activate the same stress response as when I experienced the trauma.

Think about it. When you're sitting at home with family and friends (who you feel safe with), and all of a sudden a friend of yours runs up behind you and playfully grabs you, what's your reaction? You jump, and probably scream a little. But why? You know that you are with people who wouldn't hurt you, in a place where you feel safe, so, naturally, you shouldn't be afraid. But your body remembers that when someone runs up behind you, it probably means that your mean cousin is going to push you into the mud or your annoying uncle is about to pick you up and throw you into the pool. Regardless of what your mind may know about your safe surroundings, your body's memory tells you to jump when someone grabs you.

Understanding the way my body stores memories of the trauma has been a powerful tool for working through triggers. A perfect example is orgasming – something I will talk about in much more depth in the next chapter. For now, I'll share this story.

I have the morning off and I am laying in bed when an exciting thought pops into my head: *I have time to masturbate!* I decide to spend the morning making myself feel good. I relax into my bed and begin masturbating. I orgasm, get out of bed, and start getting ready for work. I make breakfast, I get dressed, I brush my teeth, but I suddenly become aware of a negative feeling that has been surrounding me since I finished masturbating.

"Why am I feeling like this?" I ask. Almost immediately, this thought pops into my head: *My body attributes the sensation of orgasming with abuse.* When I experience an orgasm in the present, all the feelings of guilt, shame, disgust, feeling dirty, and being afraid that my body remembers feeling when I was forced to orgasm during the abuse are activated in the present moment.

Although the act of masturbation is intended to bring pleasure, my body has stored the experience of orgasming as an emotionally painful experience. We've already talked about how to work through triggers. Now, I want to talk about redefining touch in order to release stored memories and heal emotional wounds.

I never experienced good touch in a non-sexual way. Of course, I had been with partners who loved me in a completely committed, safe, and respectful way, but I don't count those here because part of my relationship with my partners was a sexual one. Therefore, all that good touch was still within the context of a sexual relationship. I have never experienced good touch in a non-sexual context. People with healthy, loving parents experience good touch through hugs after a long day at school or cuddling during family movie nights. I only experienced touch in a violating way.

I am in my bed and Lisa begins kissing me. I don't like it. It feels weird. It's like what I see in the movies when girls and boys kiss. I don't think moms are supposed to kiss kids like that. I am uncomfortable and I pull away.

"It's okay," Lisa says. She is so nice and comforting. She starts touching me in my private areas. I really don't like it, and I try to make her stop. "This is what we're supposed to do," she says, "This is okay. This is what loving parents do."

Lisa's touch was always violating, but she attempted to mask the abuse with fake maternal kindness. This manipulation made touch even more confusing for me. Trying to decipher which touch was good and which was bad became too much, so I developed the belief that I couldn't trust any touch. My body stored touch as a sensation that leads to abuse, pain, confusion, betrayal, and fear. As an adult, away from the abuse, I needed to teach my body what good touch was.

So, Where the Heck do You Start With That?

Just like we did at the beginning of the book, we need to break it down Barney-style. Good versus bad is a fundamental concept that children begin learning the moment they are born. But abuse completely distorts the meaning of good versus bad, especially in regards to touch. I can rationalize good versus bad all day, but my body - and the memories it holds - has no idea which touch is good or bad. As far as my body is concerned, all touch is dangerous. For this reason, I have to go back to the very foundations of good versus bad and relearn the difference between good and bad touch.

Start by Defining What *Good* Touch and *Bad* Touch Mean to You

Good Touch

Touch that doesn't scare me. Touch that makes me feel valued and cherished and excited and close in a loving and safe way. Touch that also makes me feel uplifted, comforted, and supported.

Bad Touch

Touch that makes me uncomfortable. This includes someone creepily pushing up against me on a crowded bus, someone getting too close to me at the bar, physical pain, and unhealthy, nonconsensual sexual advances. Touch that makes me feel used or hurt.

Put Them in Categories

Defining what good touch and bad touch meant to me was a great start. But I needed to do more. I needed to acknowledge that the touch I experienced in the past was bad. This sounds obvious but, remember, we're breaking it down Barney-style. Yes, I knew that my adult self could distinguish between good and bad touch, but there was a part of me that was always hesitant about touch. Rationally, I knew that my best friend's mom hugging me was good touch, but because of past experiences, there was always a part of me that felt unsure. Tim and Lisa told my little kid selves that the touch they experienced was good—that it was love. Other times, they told me that the touch I was experiencing was punishment. So how do I sort through a lifetime of mixed messages and confusion? I do just that. I start sorting.

Start by listing three examples of good touch and bad touch from your past and how you felt during those moments.

Let's start with good touch memories:

- **Good Touch:** When my high school softball team ran onto the field to lift me into a huddle after I made a great play.
  - *feelings*: Connected, elated, proud, happy, excited.

- **Good Touch:** When my best friend's mom kissed me on the forehead and gave me a gift at my fifth grade birthday party.
  - *feelings*: Cared for, happy, excited, thought of, seen.

- **Good Touch:** When my favorite teacher hugged me after college graduation.
  - *feelings*: Loved, recognized, valued, I felt she was proud of me, which made me feel proud of myself, congratulated, hopeful, safe.

Here are a few of my bad touch memories:

- **Bad Touch:** When Tim encouraged me to affectionately cuddle him, but told me to keep my head in his lap.
  - *feelings*: Uncomfortable, devalued, afraid, confused.

- **Bad Touch:** When lisa gave me back rubs under my shirt and tried to touch my breasts.
  - *feelings*: Scared, gross, ashamed, helpless, powerless, confused.

- **Bad Touch:** When the bully on my second grade soccer team tried to kick me repeatedly in the shins.
  - *feelings*: Angry, pure unadulterated rage (I ended up beating him up).

Categorizing my memories of touch helps me to redefine the lines that Lisa and Tim attempted to blur. It also helps me to enjoy touch that I couldn't before. For example, one of my bad touch memories involved Lisa giving me back rubs under my shirt. It makes me uncomfortable because she usually tried to touch my butt or breasts during the back rub. Because of my previous experiences, back rubs from my partner can sometimes feel uncomfortable because my body, on the cellular level, has stored back rubs as bad touch. Categorizing my memories allows me to redefine touch that I enjoy. It allows me to place "back rubs from Lisa" into the bad touch category and "back rubs from my partner" into the good touch category. This helps me separate the two touches and disconnect the new good touch from any bad past memories.

One of the common feelings I experienced during my bad touch memories growing up was confusion. I was confused because my gut was telling me that this touch was bad, but Lisa or Tim or other family members told me that this type of touch was normal or acceptable or good. Categorizing my memories re-establishes my confidence in myself. Because of the consistent confusion I experienced as a kid, I spent years of my adult life not believing that I was able to distinguish between good and bad touch, and fearing and avoiding all touch as a result. Recalling a memory and firmly telling myself, "This touch was given with love and support," or, "This touch wasn't okay and I'm sorry I experienced it," validates that I do absolutely have the ability to know which touch is good and which touch is bad. The lesson that Tim and Lisa attempted to teach me, that "Whatever touch we use is acceptable," has no power over me or my distinction between good and bad touch anymore.

Your Turn

Think of three memories that you have during which you experienced good touch. Remember how you felt during those moments. Did you feel safe? Did you feel happy or excited or supported or connected? Take a minute to close your eyes and really recall that memory and all the feelings you experienced in those moments. List your good touch memories and the emotions you associate with those memories.

If you are comfortable, do the same with your bad touch memories. Once you have finished, take the time to read these lists out loud. Again, this next part may sound a bit childish, but we're really working to validate and heal those child parts of yourself, so go with me on this.

Read your list of good touch out loud and say, "These are examples of good touch. Touch like this is what I will accept in my life." Then read your list of bad touch out loud and say, "These are examples of bad touch. This is the type of touch that I should never have had to experience. It wasn't okay that I experienced them. This is the type of touch that I will not accept in my life."

So, we defined good and bad touch. Now, how the heck do we *experience* good touch? Here are a few methods that worked for me. Check them out and see if any are a fit for you.

Take a Yoga Class

My relationship with my sister was strained for a long time as a result of the abuse. Because we were forced by Lisa and Tim to abuse each other, touching each other as adults was triggering. Simply hugging each other made us both uneasy.

I am back in the city I grew up in to attend a funeral for a woman who was like a mother to my sister and I while we were growing up. I am sitting next to my sister during the funeral service. We both start crying, and I want so badly to hold her hand and comfort her. But I can't. I can't touch her without feeling violated and scared. I am devasted. I hate that I cannot comfort or be comforted by someone I love so much.

The next day, I attend my sister's yoga class. This is the first time I get to attend a class that she is teaching. Halfway through the class, she announces that she is going to walk around the classroom and gently adjust anyone who needs help getting into their yoga position. As I lay on my mat, Sarah kneels down next to me. I keep my eyes closed while she gently adjusts my feet and my legs. She moves to my arms and when she gets to my hands, she stops and gently holds my hand. I can feel her love. I start crying. This is the first time we've been able to touch each other without fear.

That is the power of good touch. It allows you to experience the touch of another human being who simply wants to make you feel good.

Try a Reiki Session

My therapist is also a Reiki practitioner and it was actually her idea for me to discover what good touch is. She suggested that I schedule a Reiki session with her. The beauty about Reiki is that it can be done through touch or by simply hovering your hands over the body. So, if you're not comfortable with someone touching you, they don't have to. I was comfortable with my therapist and allowed her to touch me during our sessions.

As I lay on the table, my therapist places her hands on each of my chakras and tells me how great each one is. When she gets to my heart, she places her hands near my heart and says, "You have a beautiful, big, loving heart." I feel myself getting teary-eyed.

I never had a mother hold me while saying loving things to me. Experiencing mother energy hold me and acknowledge the beauty within me was powerfully healing. There were moments when she simply held my head and I could feel her sending loving energy to me.

Get a Massage

If Reiki isn't your thing, try getting a massage. Allow yourself to be touched, feel good, and know that the touch you're experiencing is just that - good, healing touch.

Ask Your Friends for a Hug

I read an article that said that we need four fifteen-second hugs a day for survival. We need eight fifteen-second hugs a day for maintenance and, we need twelve fifteen-second hugs a day for growth. Hugs have also been linked to lower blood pressure, decreased stress hormones, and an increase in oxytocin. Even something as simple as a pat on the back or a handshake is processed by the reward center in the central nervous system, so your mood will improve. I prefer the hugs, but if handshakes are your thing, shake away!

Cuddle a Pet

I, unfortunately, am allergic to cats and dogs – so allergic that I break out in hives if I don't wash my hand within two minutes of petting them. However, during times of extreme need for some loving contact, I have been known to tightly cuddle a cat or puppy with complete disregard for my impending hive breakout. Good touch does not have to come from humans. Simply holding a living creature who wants nothing more than to love and be loved by you can be a very powerful example of good touch. Heck, get a plant for some hugs if pets aren't your thing.

Lovingly Touch Yourself

For a long time, I couldn't caress my own arms or touch my own hands without cringing or even wanting to cry. Whenever I did try to touch myself, I would either be immediately triggered by memories of past bad touch, or I would remember examples of good touch from past partners— either way, I had no examples of good touch from myself. I realized that the only examples of touch that I had were from other people. *I have to change this*, I thought.

So I closed my eyes and focused only on me. I held my own hands and said, "This is what it feels like to hold hands." I felt love and I knew that this touch was safe. I now have this example of safe and loving touch to pull from for the rest of my life. Shortly after I did this, I was dancing alone in my apartment – as we all do. As I danced, I slowly caressed my arms. A few moments passed before I realized what I had just done. *Maybe it's just a fluke*, I thought. I cautiously tried again. I lovingly and gently caressed my arms as I danced. I was doing it! I was touching my arms and it didn't make me want to cringe or cry. In fact, the touch felt great.

Learning what good touch was, for myself with my own body, has allowed me to touch myself in ways that I couldn't before. If you're up for it, try creating examples of good touch with and for yourself. Start slow, with a touch you know will feel comfortable.

Another wonderful form of self-touch is masturbation. But that deserves it's own chapter, so here we go!

Masturbate

Woo! I said the word "masturbate!" I have successfully made everyone uncomfortable. But I'm not going to use some cutesy made-up word to allude to masturbation—doing so reaffirms the fact that masturbation is something we should be uncomfortable talking about or embarrassed to engage in. I want you to be so comfortable with your body and with the knowledge that you deserve to experience healthy, beautiful, incredible pleasure. The word "masturbation" should elicit feelings of excitement and pride instead of discomfort, embarrassment, or shame. So I'm sticking with "masturbation!"

Here's why masturbation is so important to me:

Sex was not something that I could jump into with abandon and just enjoy. Unfortunately, what others consider foreplay, I considered time I needed to spend convincing myself that I was safe and that I could have sex without feeling abused. While I was kissing my partner and he was happily visualizing me naked, I was telling myself, "It's okay, you're safe. If you don't want to do this, you totally don't have to. No problem. It's totally up to you. You're safe. You're okay…" That sucked. Having to pep-talk myself into feeling comfortable having sex has always sucked, and I always wanted to change my perception of sex, but, until recently, I never knew how.

I always viewed sex as something that happened to me. Even when I wanted to have sex in my adult life, I still felt as if my body was being taken by the man I was with. I viewed the act of a man inserting his penis into me as dominance, and me receiving his penis as a weakness or a loss of power. With this kind of view, how could sex ever truly feel enjoyable? It couldn't. It never felt fulfilling or empowering or connective. It always felt like a power struggle. Even with partners who I loved and who loved me, I found it difficult to associate sex with anything but bad touch, especially orgasming.

I am going to talk about something that many people struggle to discuss, and that is orgasming during abuse. It's common and needs to be talked about. Survivors are often ashamed of the orgasm because they think that it means that they enjoyed the abuse. *Hell no.* This is not the case at all. Orgasming is a natural bodily reaction that occurs after specific nerves are stimulated. In many cases, orgasms are uncontrollable. I orgasmed during abuse. It's terrible, not because of any fault of my own, but because I now associate the beautiful experience of orgasming with feelings and memories of shame and violation.

Until I was an adult, my body never learned how to orgasm within a positive, consensual context. During the eighteen years that I experienced abuse, my body learned to orgasm only within an abusive context. For this reason, when I masturbated as an adult or had sex with a partner, I often had to imagine different scenarios in order to orgasm. I had to think about being forced into sexual acts, or being coerced by someone older or gross looking, or being held down or verbally degraded. I hated this. It made me feel like I was abusing myself all over again. I felt completely ashamed and hurt by myself, and I felt disconnected from my partner.

The reason is unfortunate, but it makes sense. The only way for me to survive the abuse was to mentally escape it. I did that by imagining that it wasn't Lisa or Tim abusing me, but that it was someone or something else. So, I learned to dissociate during the abuse—to mentally remove myself from my body and the situation. I pictured being with an old doctor who was coercing me while I was in his office, or a gross old man who jerks off while his dog licked my clitoris, or a chair somehow coming to life and forcing me to be sexual with it. In a really sad and fucked up way, it was less emotionally damaging to experience abuse through a stranger I imagined than it was to consciously accept that the abuse was happening by Lisa or Tim.

I'm eleven years old and staying in the house alone. Lisa and Tim are gone and my sister is at a school event. The house is quiet and dark.

Someone is going to sneak into the house and rape me, I think. I feel scared and powerless. *I don't have any chance of defending myself against him,* I think. *I should just prepare myself to want it,* I conclude.

So, I begin to masturbate while thinking of the rape.

My boundaries were so violated by the abuse that I believed that convincing myself that I "wanted it" was the only way to protect myself from the fear of being raped. I thought that if I could get myself to be turned on before the rape happened then I could be less afraid while it was happening, instead of feeling like I was in Hell again. *If I convince myself to "enjoy" it, I can survive.* Doing this made me feel safer and, for a long time, I thought that was okay. Now, I wish I could travel back in time, shield my past self in light, and hold me until I realized what true safety was. (And I can, through past self-work!)

I was eleven years old at the time of this memory, but masturbating and imagining abusive scenarios as a way to prepare myself for abuse began when I was in second grade, at eight years old. These complex survival mechanisms and the wounds that caused them don't go away by themselves. I was well into my twenties before I finally discovered how to begin healing those wounds and releasing those survival tactics.

I will be honest and say that not imagining abusive scenarios while masturbating or having sex has been one of my biggest challenges. When I first started writing this chapter, I had a list of steps on how to masturbate in an empowering way. Then I caught myself and thought, *Are you serious? These haven't worked for you. Be honest. That's the whole point of this book.* So, here it goes.

Even now that I am away from the abuse and masturbating on my own or having sex with a loving partner, my mind and body often instinctively return to what I know: I remove myself from my body and send myself to another place, with someone else. But I don't want to have to picture something that makes me feel re-traumatized in order to orgasm. I want to be able to look at my partner while we make love. I want to be able to touch him and be touched by him and know that I am safe enough to be present. I want to teach my mind and body what good touch is, and how to be turned on by it. By now, I have come to accept that the path to true change can't come from anywhere else but within me, so I decided to embark on a trial and error journey to healthy, fulfilling masturbation.

My first thought was to become a sex expert. If I knew everything there was to know about sex, then maybe I would never feel powerless during sex again. So I read every book and article, and took every magazine quiz I could find. I even enrolled in a Human Sexuality class at my university and spent the semester analyzing and discussing the physiology of human sexual systems and the psychological aspects of sexual intimacy.

Soon, I could debate the pros and cons of the sexual evolution theory while showing a guy where my clitoris was and writing an essay on the biochemical responses that occur when we are attracted to someone. But all this knowledge still could not make me feel safe during sex. I still didn't know how to feel comfortable in my body, how to view sex as something I could enjoy instead of protect myself during, how to discover what I enjoyed during sex and then articulate that to my partner. Yes, I knew everything there was to know about human sexual anatomy, but

I still didn't know how to heal my mental and energetic wounds around sex. So if sex-ed wasn't the answer, what was?

My second thought was, *Hey, let's try to overcome this through masturbation!* This seemed like a brilliant idea. If I could learn to masturbate and orgasm while thinking of a loving partner, I should totally be able to orgasm and enjoy sex with an actual loving partner! *Okay,* I thought, *Just masturbate and think about being with a loving partner. Do that a few times and my whole thought process will be reversed. Piece of cake!*

So, I tried it. I tried it for the first three minutes while masturbating. Those three minutes turned to nine, which turned to twelve, which soon turned to twenty-two and I still wasn't even close to orgasming. Finally, I gave up and reverted back to old negative thoughts and orgasmed in about sixty seconds. I felt terrible, again. I tried the same process while having sex with my partner. I would feel myself starting to dissociate but I would catch myself, *This is Ben. You love him, he loves you. This is you and him connecting. You are here, not anywhere else.* And I would be proud of myself because I was doing the whole connecting to your partner while having sex thing. *Yeah, I totally got this!* I would think. Then my vagina would start to get dry and it would feel like it was taking forever for me to want to orgasm. I would become self-conscious that it was "taking too long" for me to orgasm. Eventually, I would revert back to old negative thoughts to orgasm and just get it all over with, or I would just stop the whole thing and give up for the day. Either way, I would finish feeling terrible.

My third thought was to involve my partner. I knew that feeling loved and safe was a necessary foundation for me to feel comfortable during sexual intimacy. *So why not be honest about my struggle with my partner? Perhaps that will take us to a deeper level of emotional intimacy and a magic doorway of sexual pleasure and intimacy will open for me.* So, I tried it. I told him that I struggled to remain present during sex. I told him that, because of the abuse, I imagined abusive scenarios when we were together in order to orgasm. And he responded beautifully. He was completely up for finding ways to support and love me through this process. While we made love, he would even stop, look me in the eyes, and say, "I love you, we're here now. Be here with me, okay?" And I felt loved. I felt supported, connected, and held... and then I would get dry again, and revert back to my old habits to orgasm.

I felt hopeless. *Why wasn't this working?* I recognized my patterns —the biggest first step. I understood the wounds that these patterns came from—the second step. I was touching my clit and thinking about positive things, and having sex with a loving partner who I loved back. *So, why the fuck wasn't this working?*

I was focusing on the thing that I wanted to fix - masturbation and sex - instead of focusing on what I *needed* to fix in order to healthfully masturbate and have sex: my deep wounds caused by sexual trauma. I was missing the most important step: healing my wounds.

So, how the hell do I do that?

It wasn't until I started a meditation series that I found through an Instagram advertisement for fifteen dollars called "Releasing the Grip of Past Lovers" that I discovered how. At the time, I was doggy paddling through some serious emotions in regards to my ex and other men in my life, so the idea of releasing the grip of old lovers was very enticing. When I clicked on the description of the series, I was even more intrigued. Before we even got to old lovers, the first half of the meditations focused on getting to know your "pelvic bowl" and your "yoni guardian." ("Yoni" is another term for vagina). The guide talked about aligning with my true self and healing parts of myself in places I didn't even know were parts. "Alright, let's do this," I said as I clicked on the pay button and figured if it was all crap, I was only out fifteen bucks.

There were many significant moments throughout the meditations, but here are the three concepts that, quite frankly, saved me:

I Have a Pelvic Bowl and It Is Sacred

Did you know that you have a pelvic bowl? Every woman does. Your pelvic bowl is a sacred space that lovingly holds your reproductive and sexual organs, your lower digestive and urinary organs, all of the vascular and lymphatic structures, the nerves and sensitive tissues of your clitoris, the muscles of your pelvic floor, and more. *How powerful is that!?* It's like a shrine for your femininity because you're a sacred goddess and your organs and tissues deserve a freaking shrine!

Your pelvic bowl is your root. Your root holds the energy associated with your core identity. Meaning, this space holds the energy that contributes to how you view yourself.

We often think of energy as a hippy concept that isn't tangible or real, but energy exists in every living being. Our energy is a restorative life force that flows throughout our bodies. Our pelvic bowls contain a unique energy flow of their own that connects with and affects the energy flow throughout the rest of our bodies. The energy of our pelvic bowls can become blocked or stagnant as a result of heartbreak, emotional burden, or trauma; and this stagnancy can begin to affect our core identities, the foundations of how we view ourselves, others, and the world. Healing the wounds in my pelvic bowl and restoring its natural energy flow has completely transformed the way I identify with myself, and how I view and experience intimacy.

Before I discovered my pelvic bowl, I felt lost. I knew that I needed to heal wounds caused by sexual trauma, but I had no idea where to begin. My pelvic bowl gave me a starting point. For the first time in a long time, I was hopeful that I truly could heal.

Spoiler alert: I did heal and I am still healing like a pro. You can heal to, so let's get started:

Find Your Pelvic Bowl

I am focusing largely on the energy of your pelvic bowl, but this bowl is also an anatomically accurate structure. Your pelvic bowl begins at the top of your hip bones and moves all the way down to your pelvic floor, encapsulating all the aforementioned organs and tissues.

Note: Even if you have had a hysterectomy or were born without certain reproductive organs, your pelvic bowl still holds energies of these organs. The full female energy system and organ energies still sacredly dwell within your pelvic bowl.

Explore Your Pelvic Bowl

Take three deep breaths in with the present moment, and out with everything else. On your last exhale, imagine that you're sitting on a pebble that is gently floating down from the top of your head all the way down to the bottom of your pelvic floor. You're here. You've reached your pelvic bowl. Say hello. How does your pelvic bowl feel? It's okay if it doesn't feel good right now, or if you don't feel anything. You may need to return a few times before you start to feel energy here again.

Once you're in your pelvic bowl, take a lap around the perimeter of your bowl. Notice any places that are blocked or caved in. What does your pelvic bowl look like?

The first time I did this meditation, my pelvic bowl was dark and dusty and it had old boards nailed everywhere as if someone had tried to either close things up permanently or fix things in a hurry. As I continued to walk around, I discovered that there were also many inflamed areas and even infected sores and wounds. At first sight, it was scary to even look at - there were so many years filled with pain that caused those wounds. It was not somewhere I felt safe or happy, but I knew it could be, which leads me to the next step.

Heal Your Pelvic Bowl

Now you are going to smooth out your pelvic bowl. Take another lap around your pelvic bowl. This time, smooth and heal any areas that need to be healed by placing both your hands on that area and sending love into it. I took my hands and imagined that as I ran them against my pelvic bowl, blue soothing light smoothed the areas. I walked all across my pelvic bowl, soothing the inflamed skin until my entire pelvic bowl was smooth and soft and welcoming. It glowed with soothing, pale blue light.

Everything does not have to be perfect right now. There may be tunnels that lead to other places or areas that just won't seem to heal. That's okay. The more you visit your pelvic bowl, the more these areas will heal. For now, lay down in the middle of your pelvic bowl. I imagine a little bean bag chair in the middle of my bowl that I curl up in and am held by. Your pelvic bowl is the safest area in the world. Your pelvic bowl was designed to hold and protect your most sacred femininity. Yes, maybe it was hurt in the past, but that's because you had no idea that it existed, therefore, it could not be used. But now that you are aware of your pelvic bowl, its power is indomitable. You can return here anytime you want and you will be held and kept safe. Welcome to your pelvic bowl.

I Have a Yoni Guardian and She Is a Badass

Within our pelvic bowl, lives our yonis. And our yonis have a guardian. This guardian is like a badass gatekeeper for our vaginas. She decides what she will and will not accept.

My first thought was, *What about abuse? If my yoni guardian decides what to accept and what to reject, where was she then?* I was actually upset by the idea of the yoni guardian - clearly, she failed me. It took me a while of reflection to realize that my yoni guardian had always been there, and did, in fact, protect me. No, she could not stop rape. But she absolutely protected the essence of my body and spirit from being affected by the abuser. She protected my energy, my pelvic bowl, and my core identity from being destroyed by abusive energy.

I am sitting in the gynecologist's office. I just started dating my first boyfriend, and I am trying to be a responsible college student by going to the doctor and getting birth control. After a lot of research, I decide that I want an IUD—a form of birth control that they insert into your uterus. This is my second visit because the doctor couldn't successfully insert the IUD during my last appointment. She just tried for the third time today, but it isn't working.

"I have inserted hundreds of IUDs in my career, and I have never encountered a cervix as tight as yours," she says. " It won't allow me to insert it."

I'm confused and upset. "Is that it then?" I ask.

"That's it for the IUD," my doctor says, "but we can schedule another appointment and talk about other options."

I leave the office, but I can't stop thinking about what the doctor said. I imagine my cervix being like, *Nope, not today, IUD!* But why?

Then, it hits me. *Holy shit. My cervix is a badass!* I realize. My cervix has spent years evolving to protect me during the abuse. My cervix essentially closed in order to protect me from pregnancy during abuse. Not only that, but it refused to allow any abusive energy to enter into my body.

That is the power of my yoni guardian. From the time I was a child, my guardian found ways to literally transform the biology of my body to protect me from damage that abuse could have caused.

One of my bullshit thoughts is that I can't tell the difference between good people who will love me and bad people who will hurt me. I was hurt by people who were supposed to love me as family, and I have been hurt by exes. So, I started to believe that I will always choose to love people who will just end up hurting me. One of the most powerful things I learned about my yoni guardian is that she knows the truth in any situation. Even when our egos or bullshit thoughts try to convince us otherwise, our guardian always knows the truth. The energy of my pelvic bowl flows through me and connects everything it holds: my root, my core identity, my all-knowing intuition, and my yoni guardian are all connected. Even when ego tells me that I am not capable of identifying who is and who is not trustworthy, my guardian knows the truth and she communicates directly with my intuition. I know, deep down, in that sacred space of my pelvic bowl, which energy to let in and which to discard, and my guardian will always be there to help me do that.

Receiving Is My Superpower

The core of my issues around sex was I believed that sex - my vagina receiving a penis - was weakness. I believed that the very act of a penis entering my vagina meant that the man was dominant and I, the woman, was powerless. This belief is why simply masturbating while thinking about having sex with my partner or some other nice guy didn't solve my problems. No matter how present I was with my partner, I still had a skewed perception of sex as a powerless battle. It wasn't until I got to know my pelvic bowl, discovered my yoni guardian, and understood the true, powerful nature of receiving that I could stop viewing my vagina as something I needed to constantly protect. Sex was not something I had to guard myself against. It was simply something I could choose or not choose to receive. In fact, receiving is my superpower.

Receiving, whether it be receiving love from a friend, receiving gifts from anyone, or receiving a lover's penis, is not a weakness. In fact, receiving is a natural part of our divine feminine essence and it's a freaking superpower! Receiving is a superpower in countless ways, but in the context of sex, I have the power to allow a penis to visit my most sacred space, and within that space this penis experiences absolute pleasure. That is powerful! I realized that the very thing I thought meant that I was weak - receiving - is actually one of the most powerful gifts I have.

Discover Your Superpower

Now you're going to connect with your ability to safely and powerfully receive. We are going to connect with Mother Nature. Mother Nature also has the divine feminine superpower of receiving. She will receive anything that you give her. She then takes it, no matter how toxic it is, and she transmutes it into light, love, and nutrients for those willing to receive.

Close your eyes, take three deep breaths in with the present moment and out with everything else. Imagine that you're sitting on a pebble that is gently traveling from the top of your head all the way down to the bottom of your pelvic bowl. Say hello and check in with your pelvic bowl.

Once you two are caught up, imagine an opening in the floor of your pelvic bowl. Imagine a stream of light from your pelvic bowl, through your cervix, and out through your yoni, into the Earth. Imagine that the stream of light travels all the way down to the core of the Earth. You are now connected with Mother Earth. You can talk to her for a bit if you'd like. Now, take everything that is concerning you, any obstacles you feel like have been insurmountable up to this point and surrender them to Mother Earth. Imagine all of them traveling through your stream of light and into the Earth. Ask Mother Earth to take these concerns and transform them. Notice how she receives them all without fear. In fact, she is light and happy the entire time. Notice how you feel when you surrender those concerns. Now, if you are comfortable, ask to receive love, light, and whatever Mother Nature knows you need. Take a deep breath in, and on your exhale, imagine all the light, love, and emotional nutrients you need traveling up through your stream of light into your pelvic bowl. How do you feel?

I am not going to lie. This part was difficult for me at first. I really did not like the idea of anything entering me through my yoni. It helped me to imagine my light connection to Earth as gold sparkles floating in a slow, stream-like fashion. Know that your guardian is there and she will not allow anything toxic to enter your pelvic bowl. Believe that receiving is your superpower. Nothing is entering you without your consent. You are powerfully allowing your body to receive what you want through the stream of light you have created. Once you are satisfied, thank Mother Earth and allow the stream of light to dissipate. You may imagine the opening from your pelvic bowl to your cervix gently close. Take a deep breath in, and on the exhale, come back to the present.

You may connect with Mother Earth at any time. Whenever you have an emotion or story or memory you need to release, ask Mother Earth to accept and transform it, then surrender it to her. You may also ask Mother Earth to provide you with any support you need. Receiving is your superpower, so ask for what you need and know that it is safe to receive.

Putting It All Together

After connecting with my pelvic bowl, I felt truly connected to my body and energy for the first time in my life. I didn't feel like my vagina was something I needed to protect or avoid, and I didn't feel like being feminine was a weakness. I understood that embracing the energy of my pelvic bowl, allowing myself to touch and connect with my body, and receiving support and love was not only incredibly powerful but also safe. I was no longer afraid that doing so was opening me up to more pain or vulnerability. I decided that it was time to try masturbating again, but I wanted to do things differently this time.

I close my eyes and imagine myself floating down into my pelvic bowl. When I arrive, I lay down in my soft bean bag chair in the center of my pelvic bowl. I feel safe, held, protected, and free here. Nothing in the world can access me here. This is truly my space.

I think about all the times guys have asked me, "What do you like?" or, "What do you want me to do?" My answer is always a nervous, "I don't know..." followed by feelings of discomfort and awkwardness. I always thought that I answered that way because I was put on the spot and didn't know what I wanted in that moment, but I'm realizing now that I don't actually have any freaking idea what I like sexually.

I know from the meditations that I have struggled all my life with feeling good while having sex with a partner, so I don't want to try fantasizing about having sex with another person right now.

"So, where do I go from here?" I ask my pelvic bowl.

"Just think of things that make you feel good," she responds. I am surprised by the simplicity of this answer.

"Okay, I can do that," I reply.

I gently rub my clitoris and start imagining myself in different outfits that I absolutely love—the clothing that makes me feel the most sexy and goddess-like. *Wow, I feel pretty awesome,* I think. I continue. *I want to figure out what I like sexually,* I think. *Well, I know I like when someone kisses my nipples,* I think. *I'll start there.*

As I sit, relaxed in my bean bag chair, I imagine lips gently sucking on my nipple. The lips aren't attached to anyone or anything—I'm not ready for that yet. For now, they're just lips. I've heard about people liking when someone sucks on their toes, so I'm like, *Hey, let's give it a try.* But imagining lips sucking on my toes feels creepy to me, so I imagine suction cup things that suck my toes. And that feels really good, too. I notice that I'm getting turned on. I know that I love when partners kiss my neck, so I imagine lips kissing my neck. I notice that I am rubbing my clitoris so slowly - more slowly than I have ever done before - and it is definitely working. *Wow,* I think, *so I like rubbing my clit slowly. Awesome, good to know.*

I continue imagining different things. Some turn me on, others, not so much. I take note of what I like, and it's exciting. For the first time in my life, I am learning, for myself, what I like! Then, it happens. I orgasm. But not a regular orgasm. This is, straight up, the best orgasm I have ever had. Then I keep going! *What?!* I think out loud, "I never keep going!" I always stop after one orgasm and move on. But I continue gently massaging my clit at the same speed and I feel something incredible building. "Am I going to cum again?!" I excitedly and nervously exclaim. I think I have maybe kind-of-orgasmed twice with a partner once before in my life, but I wasn't ever sure if it actually happened and I decided that it was impossible for me to orgasm more than once. Within seconds, a powerful, incredibly pleasurable second orgasm washes over me and it is the most satisfying, empowering, freaking beautiful sexual experience I have ever had. I laugh and shriek with joy and hold myself. THAT is what masturbation and sex should be and can be every single time.

That moment was truly life-changing for me. Not just because I orgasmed twice - although, that was awesome - but because I realized that my sexual experience belongs to me. I choose which energy comes in and which energy goes out. I choose what I think about. I choose to connect with my pelvic bowl and yoni as parts of my core identity—not injured, disconnected body parts that I need to protect. From this moment forward, I am in control of my own sexual experience, and I am capable of enjoying every second of it.

This type of masturbation takes a little more time at the beginning. I'm not just rubbing my clit, cumming, and then going to work. I need to ground into my pelvic bowl and connect with myself more deeply. I need to have an ongoing conversation with myself as I masturbate. I touch myself slowly and allow for build-up. This wasn't always something I felt like doing. There were times when I just wanted to think about whatever I needed to think about, orgasm in sixty seconds, and then move on with my day. But I knew that this wasn't just about orgasming. I was re-wiring my brain to enjoy healthy, beautiful, consensual sexual experiences.

Most importantly, I was connecting with myself while masturbating and creating a foundation of self-love. I was saying, "Hey, I love you so much, and how you feel when you masturbate or have sex is important. You deserve to enjoy this, so let's figure out what helps you feel good." My point is, you're not always going to feel like doing this, but commit to it. It's been over a year since I started this healing work, and everything about how I view and experience masturbation and sex has transformed. I am so incredibly proud and relieved to say that:

1. I no longer have to enter into a meditative, focused state in order to masturbate. Masturbating in a way that builds me up and brings me pleasure has become a habit, not something I have to work hard to experience.

2. I am able to masturbate while thinking of being with a loving partner. After creating the foundations of self-love and healing, I absolutely feel safe imagining being with, and actually being with, a partner during sex.

3. I no longer crave the type of stimulation I did before. I am not tempted to think of degrading scenarios while masturbating or having sex. In fact, if I do think about those things, they actually turn me off. I actually tested myself because I couldn't believe that it was real. While I masturbated, I said, "But for real, aren't you turned on by thinking about [insert scenario that I used to use to orgasm]." "Ugh, no, I don't like that," I quickly responded. And I meant it. I really truly meant it. I was elated. I healed one of the most challenging, seemingly evasive and insurmountable wounds from my past.

No, this didn't happen overnight. This took a dedicated effort. But I can promise you that if you take the time to connect with and heal your pelvic bowl, and, when you're ready, begin masturbating with the goal of simply loving yourself and discovering what makes you feel good, you will connect with and heal the core of your sexual identity and experiences, and you will be able to experience the level of sexual pleasure and satisfaction that you want and deserve. Woo! I said "masturbation" like forty-five times throughout this chapter and we all made it! Girl, your pelvic bowl thanks you.

Stop Recreating
Your Past

*"Pay attention to your patterns. The ways you learned to
survive may not be the ways you want to continue to live."*
-Dr. Thema Bryant-Davis

"If we have been killed, my dad did it," I write on a piece of paper, but the message is written in code—a code I create and write down
on another piece of paper.

If he finds this, he will kill me, I think. *Where can I hide it?*

*Well, I can't hide the code with the letter. If Dad finds the letter and the
code, he'll be able to read it,* I think. *I can leave the code on my shelf, so police
can find it. But I need a place for the message. I need a place where investigators
will find it because they know where to look,* I think, *but it also has to be somewhere Dad won't look.*

I notice a crack in my windowsill just wide enough to fit a sliver of paper without being too noticeable.

"Perfect," I say as I move toward the window. *Pretend to be opening the window so the cameras can't see you,* I think.

I open my window as a distraction as I slide the sliver of paper into the windowsill crack.

I just hope the police can find the code and the letter, I think, as if this is a normal thought that every kid has.

There were cameras all over the house I grew up in. There were cameras in my room, cameras in the bathroom. All our conversations were recorded so my sister and I could never talk about the abuse to anyone. For the first half of my life, constant surveillance, violation of privacy, abuse, and believing that me and my sister would be murdered was as normal and everyday as packing a lunch for school. I lived in constant fight-or-flight mode. Put simply, I lived with an eighteen-year-long adrenaline rush.

The patterns I created in order to survive prolonged threats to my safety didn't simply disappear once I was away from the abuse. Although, consciously, I knew that I was finally safe, I didn't know how to shut off the hyper-alert mode. I never learned how. Even something as simple as sleeping was something I never learned to do as I always had to be conscious enough to know when someone was entering my room to hurt me.

For the first seven years after the abuse, I had to learn what peace and stability were. I didn't know how to live in peace and stability - and, if I'm being honest, I didn't want to. As unhealthy as it sounds, after living an eighteen-year-long adrenaline rush, peace and stability felt boring AF. It felt as if I had been snowboarding a 20,000 foot descent for my whole life and now I was being asked to leisurely sip afternoon tea. I was addicted to adrenaline. And because I had only ever experienced adrenaline through unhealthy, unsafe experiences, those were the only places I knew where to get my adrenaline fix from. So, I recreated my past. I spent years manifesting chaos in my life through unhealthy, unsafe, unstable situations and relationships.

"Why does this keep happening?!" Have you ever asked this question? Have you ever angry-cried in your car and cursed the Universe because another partner cheated or another boss was manipulative or the job you thought would work out fell through again? You're not going to be happy when I say this but, this keeps happening because you are creating it. We can tell ourselves and others about how desperately we want a better relationship, less manipulative bosses, more loyal friends, etc., but a few weeks later, we find ourselves in a situation that mimics the previous one almost exactly.

Now, I want to make one thing very clear before we move on. I am not and will never suggest that the abuse you have experienced is your fault. I would never imply that the abuse I experienced as a child was my fault. I will, however, adamantly preach that I have allowed all the bullshit thoughts, emotions, and stories that developed because of that abuse to continue to affect my life in negative ways. And it took me a long time to realize that all of these shitty things were happening because I was creating them. But the cool thing is, if I have the kind of power that can create these colossally shitty circumstances in my life, I also have the power to create colossally great circumstances. But we'll talk about that more a little later. First, what do I mean when I say that we are recreating our past?

We attach ourselves to our negative experiences. We become so attached to them that we shape our identity from those experiences. In doing so, it becomes impossible for us to move on from the past because we have chosen to interweave our experiences so tightly into our identities. Now, I am sure you're thinking the same thing I said when I first heard this concept, "Excuse me, but I definitely don't do that." But you do. I did, too. That's why the same shit kept happening to me over and over and over again. Remember that comfort zone thing we talked about earlier? Well, the same concept applies here.

No matter how terrible the experiences are that I have created my identity from, it is my identity. *If I let go of those experiences, who would I be?* The thought of releasing a part of who you are without knowing what you will become is terrifying. That's why we don't do it. Instead, we spend our lives preserving the identities we have created by holding on to our negative experiences and using them to recreate our pasts.

Here are three identities I created from the abuse:

I am a Victim

As a child, the only time the abuse ceased was when I was helpless. When every part of who I was seemed empty, Lisa and Tim would stop the abuse. Although not abusing someone is certainly not love, it was the closest thing I could get. So, I adopted the belief that if I was a helpless victim then I could protect myself from the abuse, someone would want to save me, and I would be loved.

When I first started dating, without even realizing it, I absolutely tied myself to a victim identity. I wanted to tell the man I was dating about the abuse I experienced so that he could feel sorry for me, hold me, take care of me, get angry for me, and fiercely protect me. In creating this identity, I constantly attracted men who were looking for someone to save; men who were overbearing, controlling, possessive, or clingy.

But relationships were not the only area that this victim identity permeated. Through this identity, I was constantly manifesting circumstances in which I was the victim. I was constantly changing jobs because every boss I had was vindictive, manipulative, and mean. I would go home and tell my boyfriend about how terrible work was, he would get angry for me and want to defend his helpless victim girlfriend, and the cycle would continue. No matter how hard I tried, I could never make enough money to cover my bills. I was always exhausting myself by commuting from one dead end job to the other multiple times a day. Things constantly went wrong. My car would break down, some unpaid bill from three years ago would resurface and I would owe five times more, etc. And why did all of these things happen? Because I wanted them to.

Of course, consciously, I wanted peace, abundance, and happiness. But subconsciously, my entire identity was based around the notion that I was a victim. If things went well and I was no longer a victim, what would happen? Where would I find a job? I had attracted men who wanted to save me. If I was no longer a victim, who would love me? Most importantly, who would I be? All of these questions seemed far scarier than the circumstances I was living in, so I continued to recreate my past.

I am Special

I survived trauma. While all my friends were being held by loving parents, I was being drugged and sexually tortured. While all my friends have a safety net within their families if they lose their jobs or decide they want to switch careers, I have only myself. I survived things that most people could never even imagine. And because of it, I am stronger, more independent, smarter, tougher, funnier, and more resilient. I am special.

That is the special identity. While all of that may seem better than the victim identity, it still traps me in my past. It still forces me to live within a perpetual state of having to overcome circumstances and struggle for things that "other" people receive easily. It's also a very sad attempt at attaching myself to some notion of superiority—a superiority that exists only through remaining attached to the trauma.

When I went a little deeper into the special identity, I found that it was also a mask for the fearful hope that there was a reason for the abuse. It's easier to accept that the abuse occurred if I can say that I am stronger, more independent, and more special than those who haven't experienced it. In a way, it temporarily took away some of the pain. Regardless, this special identity keeps me trapped. If I release my abusive past, my special-ness is gone.

I am a Lone Wolf

Another common identity that trauma survivors develop is the "lone wolf" identity: I've never had anyone, and I don't need anyone now. Everything I've survived in my life, I've survived on my own. People just weigh you down, I'm better off on my own. I am a lone wolf.

The term "lone wolf" refers to a wolf who leaves the pack - often because of aggressive actions from the pack's dominant wolves, including being picked on or physically challenged to the point that the wolf leaves the pack. *Yes, wolf, way to leave a toxic situation!*

I have heard this term many times to refer to a fiercely independent person and I always roll my eyes. Because lone wolves are not a symbol for healthy independence. They do not go on to lead successful lives on their own in the wilderness. In fact, lone wolves usually do one of three things: they attempt to join another pack, they look for a mate, or they die because they cannot survive on their own. Notice that two of the three options involve finding support with another wolf - the only other alternative is death. There is no such thing as a truly alive lone wolf.

The lone wolf mentality develops in people who have lived in unhealthy, unloving, toxic packs. The people they were supposed to be able to depend on hurt and betrayed them. So, they chose to leave the pack. *Again, yay for leaving unhealthy situations!* But instead of moving on to find a better pack or mate, the lone wolf-human develops a fear of the pack altogether. People with the lone wolf mentality aren't fiercely independent. In fact, it's the opposite. They are terrified. They have only ever witnessed a pack (family, relationships, friendships) as painful and unhealthy. Or they've witnessed overdependent pack members, so they believe that relationships come with the burden of taking care of people who give them nothing in return. For this reason, these "lone wolves" push away connection, love, and support entirely. If they do end up meeting someone who knows how to offer healthy love, they run away because experiencing this type of love is foreign to them - they don't trust it. "Lone wolves" constantly manifest overall life-struggle and dissatisfaction in relationships by either attracting unhealthy love or rejecting healthy love and support.

So how do we stop recreating our pasts?

Get VERY Real About What You Actually Want

For years, I said, "I just want things to be calm. I just want a stable job and income and a healthy, loving relationship." But I didn't. Calm was boring to me. I wanted adrenaline rushes and excitement—that was all I had ever known. It wasn't until I got very real with myself about that deep addiction to adrenaline created by the abuse that I was able to start identifying the patterns of chaos I was creating in my life.

What I truly want is a peaceful and stable life with healthy, exciting adventures. It took me over seven years to realize this, but once I did, I was able to start to recognize the difference between adrenaline created by unhealthy, unstable and fearful situations, and excitement created by fun, safe adventures. I now have peace and stability in the foundations of my life - jobs, home, relationships, friends. And this foundation of peace and stability safely holds space for healthy excitement and adrenaline-filled adventures.

What "Keeps Happening" to You?

Identify the patterns in your life. What seems to constantly pop up? Maybe it's abusive bosses or unhealthy relationships. Maybe it's financial struggle or friends who can't show up the way you need them to. Identify consistent occurrences in your life and write them down.

How may this occurrence be *connected* with your trauma?

What bullshit thought from your past is causing this situation to constantly pop up in your life? One of mine was the belief that I needed to be a victim to receive love. For this reason, everything in my life was a constant struggle. Another belief was that I could only experience adrenaline in unhealthy ways, so I sought out chaotic situations. How are the situations in your life connected with the bullshit thoughts from your past?

What Identity Have You Created?

How have you interwoven the abuse into your identity? Now, I am not talking about using your experiences to better yourself and the world. That is something wonderful and entirely different. I am talking about the ways in which we force ourselves to stay trapped in our traumatic pasts by making that past a core part of our identities. Take some time to reflect on how you've woven your trauma into your identity.

What Is Your Comfort Zone?

The scariest thing about the past is that we know it well. And because we know it, no matter how terrible it is, we are comfortable with it. Our comfort zones - the people we interact with most, the places we visit, the situations we find ourselves in - are all things we subconsciously choose based on our past.

I was comfortable with high stress, fight-or-flight situations, so that is what I gravitated towards. I grew up learning that I had no options. I did not get to choose who I wanted to be or what I wanted to do. Everything was forced on me. I was trapped. I know very well what it is like to be trapped. For this reason, I put myself in situations that trapped me - they were my comfort zone - which is funny because my greatest fear is being trapped. In theory, I will do anything possible to avoid being trapped, but deep down, being trapped was all I knew.

I also grew up learning that men are scary, that men can take whatever they want from me whenever they want. I learned to be quiet and small in order to try to stay safe while around mean men. No, I don't want assholes to be a part of my life. But because it's all I had ever known, because assholes were in my comfort zone, I gravitated towards situations with assholes.

Write It Down

Start by writing down your patterns. "I am constantly struggling financially." Then, write down the fear that is tied to your past and creating this pattern. "Because I believe that chaos is the only way to bring excitement into my life."

Write the Truth

You've exposed your pattern, the past it's connected to, and the negative belief you've developed as a result. (Yaas, girl!) Now, it's time to know the truth.

"Having stable foundations in my job, relationships, and life as a whole allow me the stability I need to go on all the exciting, healthy adventures I can imagine."

Make That Shit Your Mantra

Write it on a piece of paper and tape it to your mirror. Write it on several Post-it Notes and stick them all over your apartment. Leave yourself a voicemail or text or email with your new mantra. Recite this truth over and over and over and over again until it's so ingrained in your mind that it becomes a part of you.

Notice the Results

Your life will change. Take note of the changes you have created for yourself. Be proud.

When You're Ready,
Date Someone

"If I accept the fact that my relationships are here to make me conscious instead of happy, then my relationships become a wonderful self-mastery tool that keep re-aligning me with my higher purpose for living."
-Eckhart Tolle

I am sitting cross-legged in the corner of the library, surrounded by books. It's the summer of 2001 and I am twelve years old. The required age to work at the library is thirteen, but I begged to be allowed to volunteer, so here I am. I've just finished putting the same sticker on the same book four times in order to look busy enough that Johnny will go away.

"I think you did that one all already," Johnny says. Johnny is my coworker. He has brown hair, sun-tanned skin, and messed up teeth.

"I know what I'm doing," I say dismissively, hoping that he'll get the hint and leave. But Johnny doesn't move.

"Oh," he says as he continues to watch me put the same stickers on the same books.

While he stands next to me, I can feel my body arch and my shoulders hunch in a way that shields my breasts and deforms my shape —a pose I developed a long time ago in order to desexualize myself and avoid all unsolicited looks or touches. But he's still here, a love-struck Johnny who couldn't take a hint. I don't look up. My eyes are cemented to the books and their stickers. He continues to stand there.

I can feel my soul curling into a protective ball and I want to do the same. I want to curl up into a ball and clench myself so tightly closed that I silently explode into tiny pieces that no one can see. They'd all think that I just vanished. *I vanished, Johnny, leave me alone.* But, unfortunately, vanishing hasn't been invented yet, so I remain in front of him while he looks at me. On the verge of tears, I scream in my head, *Please! Please, stop looking at me. Just leave me alone!* (This is one of those times that I'll swoop down and comfort my past self.) I can feel him watching me, I can feel that he likes me and it inspires a level of fear and discomfort so great that it is almost paralyzing. All I can do is stay as still as possible and hold back tears.

A few days later, I am sitting at a desk down the hall from my boss Lydia's office. The thought of Johnny liking me inspires such grueling panic that I can't concentrate, so I decide to read a book about castles instead. I desperately want to talk with someone about the way I am feeling, but what would I say? I don't even understand how I'm feeling, how can I talk about it? I decide that multiple conversations with my boss about what I am learning from this castle book will suffice. My first trip to Lydia's office looks like this:

"Hey, I'm reading this book. Did you know that some castles [insert some sort of architectural castle fact here]?"

What I wanted to say was, "Lydia, I really need to talk to you."

The second trip went like this:

"Hey, okay, did you know that they had [insert some comment about castle crocodiles here]."

What I really wanted to say was, "Okay, Lydia, there is a boy here named Johnny and he likes me and I don't like it."

And with a little more time to reflect, I probably could have added, "I don't like it because it makes me uncomfortable."

"Uncomfortable" was a word that I used for a very long time. Though it never seemed to convey the level of discomfort I was experiencing, it was the only word I could come up with before I discovered these words: violated, invaded, unsafe and humiliated, terrified, exposed, trapped and unprotected. For the time being, "uncomfortable" was the word of choice.

The third trip involves something about medieval clothing, and that is when Lydia finally follows me back to the desk down the hall.

"Are you okay?" she asks. I want to cry. One, because I am so relieved that she came out to talk to me, and two, because I want so badly to tell her how I feel but I am confused and don't know how.

I want to say, "Lydia, when this boy looks at me, I feel terrified. I feel like I need to protect myself completely or something really scary is going to happen. But I don't want to feel this way and I don't know why I feel this way."

A few days prior, I had heard about porn addiction at school. All the teachers got really serious and concerned when talking about it. That emotional response stuck with me.

What I want to tell Lydia is, "I think me feeling uncomfortable with Johnny has something to do with my parents doing terrible things to me." But I don't know how to say that. So, I try to think of something to say that she will understand, something that will immediately elicit the emotional response that I need from her. I say the only thing that I believe can accurately convey the amount of fear that I am feeling.

"I think I might be addicted to porn," I blurt out.

I don't remember the rest of the conversation. I do know that I was never addicted to porn. But I needed an outlet for my emotions. Through Johnny, I was experiencing emotions that I couldn't place, but I knew they weren't supposed to be there. Because I was having difficulty understanding the emotions, I also had difficulty articulating them. As a deeply wounded child, I craved empathy, understanding, and nurturing. I couldn't get it by telling someone about my situation because I didn't even understand my situation. So, I projected my feelings onto a topic I thought people may more easily understand, in hopes that I could feel understood and empathized with in even the slightest way - even if it was because they thought I was addicted to porn.

One of the most significant parts of this memory is that I never said, "I think my dad/mom is addicted to porn." I said, "I think I might be addicted to porn." I internalized my abusive experiences and took responsibility for the bad things that were happening to me. Although I was in no way responsible for the anxiety I was experiencing as a result of the abuse, I believed that, because I was feeling bad, I must be doing bad things. Accepting responsibility for the actions of abusers and the emotions that came from those actions was something I grew up learning to do. As a kid, every year during Christmas, I just knew that Santa wasn't coming. "Was I bad this year?" I would ask while sobbing. What I didn't realize at the time was that those feelings of being bad that I was experiencing were not me actually being bad. They were my gut telling me that bad things were happening to me. But how does a kid verbalize, "I am feeling very uneasy and scared and just overall bad, but it's not my fault. It's because my parents are abusing me?" The answer is, she can't. So instead, I recognized that I was feeling bad and I came to the only conclusion a child could think of: I must be bad.

I learned to take responsibility for the emotions I felt when someone mistreated me. This pattern continued into adulthood. When people did shitty things to me, instead of connecting the hurt feelings I felt to the

the bad things they did, I accepted responsibility for my hurt and tried to figure out what I did to cause it.

Relationships will rip open unhealed wounds and leave you completely exposed to all the emotions that ooze from your past. Although I only knew Johnny for about three weeks and only had a handful of interactions with him, Johnny was my introduction to relationships. He was my first experience with having someone have a crush on me—of being seen in a way that makes me feel exposed to my deepest wounds. He showed me what it felt like to be triggered by all of my fears that developed from the abuse before I even knew what a trigger was. Simply feeling him look at me inspired a fear so powerful that I had to fight back tears and the urge to run away and hide. My journey with Johnny was fleeting, simple, and terrifying. It stayed with me for a very long time.

In fact, it wasn't until I was in college that I felt prepared to attempt to navigate relationships again. And when I say navigate, I mean dip my toes in like a four-year-old visiting a pool for the first time. I wasn't ready to jump in. I knew that. But I needed to know what a relationship was. I needed to understand my fears, my wounds, my triggers, my desires, and everything that was simultaneously pulling me towards the desire to be in a relationship, and all the emotional walls that were barricading me with fear.

My relationship history can be broken down into two categories: attempts at relationships and actual long-term relationships. Each of these journeys have become some of the most powerful tools in helping me become conscious of the ways my past affects the way I view myself, other people, and the world. They have all provided me with some serious insight into the bullshit thoughts that were completely sabotaging my ability to connect with people, the wounds that were triggered while connecting with someone romantically, how to better heal those wounds, and how to deeply connect with my own self-love in order to feel safe truly loving and being loved in return. That said, my relationship journeys didn't really feel like powerful tools at the time. In fact, while they were happening, they usually felt awkward as hell.

So, I am putting ego aside, grabbing some cake pops, and getting ready to embarrass-eat sweets while you read about my relationship history. I hope you laugh, empathize, and connect with the stories. Mostly, I hope that in reading mine, you'll lovingly learn from your own.

So, let's get started with the first category.

Relationship Attempts

Kenny

Kenny walks me back to my dorm. It's the end of our first date. I say goodnight and try as best I can to confidently walk back to my room. I turn the corner and know that I am out of sight. I am shaking so hard that I can barely breathe and my knees shake until I sit down on the floor. My heart races and I try to catch my breath as I teeter on the edge of a panic attack.

I just went on a first date, so I have to go on a second, I think. *And if I go on a second, he'll want a third, and on the third date, everyone knows we have to kiss, then he'll want more and I'll have to give it to him,* I panic. *Then I'll have to have sex with him, and I can't do that. I hate that, the idea of it makes me sick…* My thoughts continue to spiral until I blurt out, "I won't go out with him again! I don't have to do this again. He's gone and I'm safe."

Moving to another city for college helped me feel like I was finally breaking away from my past experiences. Knowing that I was in a place where contact with anyone from my past was almost impossible was like being able to breathe for the first time. Although I was still dealing with a lot of unhealed triggers and memories, I really did feel safe for the first time in my life. As I continued to feel safer, my desire for some type of connection with someone also developed. I wanted to feel liked. I wanted to feel desired. I wanted to feel sexy even. But the thought of being physically intimate still paralyzed me with fear. I decided that I needed a way to feel sexually desired by a potential partner without ever having to worry about actually committing to a relationship or being intimate. I developed what I called "sushi love."

As a film student, I even created an entire film around the concept. Sushi Love, both the film and the concept, is all about the way an incomplete piece of sushi can represent an interaction that allows you to connect with potential partners in a way that excites you but keeps them at a safe sexual distance. You have the salmon, the rice, the wasabi paste all entwined together in a deliciously promising fashion, but no seaweed wrap to hold it together. You can flirt and smile and fantasize about the possibility of being with this specific individual (the salmon, rice, and wasabi paste), but you never have to worry about actually being in a relationship (the seaweed wrap).

The key to a sushi love is to find someone who is so infatuated with you, and who is also painfully shy. The shy part is important because you need them to be so introverted that she/he could never even fathom trying to ask you out. It's the perfect situation because the interactions you have with this person will be so minimal that the possibility of even becoming close enough to have to be afraid of intimacy is almost completely eliminated.

Not following? Well, here's a story about Kenny to illustrate my sushi love theory a little more clearly. Kenny started working at our school library during my second year of college. I knew that he liked me by the way he looked at me. Every day, I went to the library, asked for a book, smiled, and watched his hand nervously shake as he handed me my class readings. I did this for months.

Kenny, the shy library guy, is the perfect candidate for a sushi love. Kenny is smaller in build but fit because he rides his bike to work every day, and everyone thinks he's a mute because he never talks. Shy, possibly mute Kenny will never be bold enough to ask me out or move this sushi love to the next level. He is perfect. So, every day, I go to the library. I ask for my books and smile as he hands them over. I walk into the library as the breeze from the automatic doors blows my hair back in slow motion and I bask in the confidence of knowing that he is watching, smitten. I sit near him with my friends and make jokes loud enough for him to hear so that he knows I'm funny. But after about five months of sushi love making, I am discontent.

Yeah, being physical with someone freaks me out, I think, *but I'm never going to know if I'm ready for a relationship until I try, right?*

I decide to try. I invite Kenny to a party I am planning.

It's the night of the party and one of the worst winter storms of the year is swirling outside. Only about five people show up. I am convinced that the night is a bust. Moments before I give up on the night, I see Kenny knocking on the window. He rode his bike through the blizzard to come to my party. We sit together in an empty party room with a couple of my friends and talk for the rest of the night. We spend the following weeks exchanging band names and songs that we like, and we even go on a few dates before I leave for the summer. We continue to talk over the phone and I know, after a couple of weeks, he is smitten. It feels wonderful!

We are in different states, hours apart, so I connect with him on the phone. I learn about his favorite movies, and we plan for our first date when I get back to school, all without the concern of physical intimacy.

Summer ends and I am back at school. As soon as I return, those familiar feelings of panic begin to surface. Everytime I receive a text from Kenny, I feel violated and uncomfortable. I resent him because every time I think of him touching me or I hear his voice, I feel trapped in something that I'm scared of. I feel forced into a relationship in which intimacy will be "required."

I have to get out, I think. *I can't be in a relationship with him. I can't kiss him. I don't want to hold his hand.* I begin to panic. *I hate him.*

Even just knowing that there are texts from him on my phone makes me feel violated, like all of my personal space is being invaded and he won't leave me alone. I feel suffocated. I want to throw my phone in a river and hide in a corner of my room and never come out. "I don't want to see him," I say out loud. "I can't see him. I have to get out. I have to get out of this!"

After a short period of avoided texts, I call Kenny and tell him that I can no longer see or talk to him.

I wrote Kenny off, saying, "I just can't be myself with him." And that was true. I couldn't be myself. I would spend the entire date so consumed by a fear of even accidentally grazing hands with him that I shut down entirely when I was around him.

Not being able to be myself stemmed, in part, from not knowing how to establish boundaries – more importantly, not knowing that I could establish boundaries. I believed that being in a relationship meant that being intimate with someone was required, whether I was ready for it or not. I didn't know that I could say, "I'm not ready to kiss yet," or, "I don't want to have sex right now." With the insanity that was my childhood, of course, I never learned that boundaries were something I had the power to create.

There was no way that I could connect with Kenny because I didn't know what relationships were. To me, a relationship meant that I was obligated to be sexually intimate whether I wanted to or not, which isn't a partnership. It is abuse. So, of course, the idea of entering into a relationship was re-traumatizing. Although it took me years to realize that a huge part of my fear of intimacy was based in the belief that I had to do things that I didn't want to do, my journey with Kenny planted the seed that I needed to heal some deep wounds and bullshit thoughts surrounding my belief about what a healthy, loving relationship really was.

Max

A year later, I met Max. During my sophomore year of college, I was invited to attend a leadership conference in Boston. Well, not quite Boston. It was actually a convent turned retreat center in the middle of a field surrounded by trees that too similarly resembled the setting of The Village. Did I mention it was in the middle of nowhere? I met my friend, Ally, who had also been invited at the airport. We took a taxi to the leadership conference building, and upon arrival, the leadership official took our bags and demanded our keys, stating, "You'll get these back at the end of the week once the conference is over." It was then that I began to plot my escape. My mood quickly changed from pessimistic but willing to pretend like I was open to the experience, to completely cynical and openly sarcastic. After four hours of unpacking and leadership activities, we were free for the rest of the night. I met up with Ally and immediately began discussing the escape plan.

"Look, Sarah (our mutual friend) lives around Boston, she can be here in an hour. She can drive up – we're barely unpacked – she'll pick us up. We'll wait by the window. We can jump out the window. It's really not that far..."

I am interrupted by a more rational Ally. "How about we just go out the door?" she asks.

"Yeah, but there are totally snipers guarding the premises. We'd never make it out," I joke.

"How about we just take a walk around for a while and see if you feel better after?" Ally suggests.

Not the response I am looking for, but we have an hour before our escape car can even arrive, so I agree. I throw my hair up in a messy bun, put on a sweatshirt and running shorts, and wear my gym shoes without socks—and wearing gym shoes without socks is gross, that's how much I didn't care. Ally and I start walking. We stop at the edge of the driveway - as far as we are sure we're allowed to go. I start warning Ally of the dangers of drinking the juice there when I see Max.

It is not love at first sight. I mean, I find him attractive but I saw him earlier that day and didn't think anything about it. The retreat center has a complex layout. While attempting to return to my room earlier that day, I ended up in the basement. As I frustratedly made my way back up the stairs, I ran into Max and said, "How the fuck do I get up to the top floor?" He, taken aback, pointed towards the ascending stairs and I, un-affected, continued up to my room. That was our first interaction. And now we were meeting again.

"Hey, are you the guy I swore at earlier?" I say as I look at him and grin.

He grins back and responds, "Yup, that's me." He walks closer to me.

"Yeah, that shit's confusing," I poignantly state.

I spend the next six days with Max. Usually, my sarcasm intimidates guys, but not Max. I am shocked by the way that he is not only not intimidated by it, but he really seems to like it. For the first time in my entire life, I am being myself with a guy, and it's so easy! We spend the week flirting, sharing sarcasm-based stories, making fun of the conference, and forming a closeness that I never thought I was capable of.

Let me pause for a moment to remind you of how severe my fears of intimacy were. Example 1: When speaking with guys, my mouth would immediately become dry. I was so terrified of the possibility of sexual or emotional intimacy that my subconscious sucked all the moisture from my mouth, rendering me literally unable to continue the conversation. Example 2: My complete and utter horror of kissing someone. Most individuals who have not kissed anyone are naturally nervous for their first time. But my fear was deeper than first-time jitters. I truly believed that I was incapable of partaking in the act. I could give the look - the look that says, "Oh, hi, let's lean in and kiss." I could then slowly lean in closer to his face. The lean in... the lean in... and then... WHAM. Finished. It was like the Berlin Wall came plummeting down from 50,000 feet above our heads and landed right between our lips. I was paralyzed, I couldn't move. My body physically would not allow me to go any farther. Before Max, I had accepted the fact that, though I may go on dates, I would never be like other people. I would never be able laugh and pull my boyfriend in close to me while we talked about how we first met. I would never be able to scratch the back of his neck the way women in movies always touch their boyfriend's necks. Closeness caused a paralyzing mix of anxiety and fear, so I accepted that closeness was something I would never have. It hurt, but I accepted it.

Getting close to Max isn't easy. I am scared every day. I am completely oozing and ready to explode with anxiety. Every day, I am tempted to say, "You know what, I'm cool, I don't need this anymore. I'm going to withdraw and hide from you." But there's a part of me that pushes me to go further. Maybe I'm just ready, or maybe I just really like Max that much. Either way, the fear of not trying to get closer to him is greater than the fear of being intimate—something I've never experienced before. For the first time in my life, I believe that if I push through this fear, something good can come from it. More importantly, for the first time in my life, I want to push through the fear.

During the conference, everyone was given mailboxes so that people could send leadership-based niceties in letter form to their fellow conference attendees.

I walk to Max's mailbox. I wrote Max a letter and am getting ready to put it in his mailbox. I know that by placing this letter in his mailbox, I am taking a step toward becoming closer with him—becoming closer means emotional closeness and, potentially, someday, physical closeness. As I walk toward his mailbox, everything in my body wants to turn, run to my room, and curl up into a ball until I vanish. But I keep walking.

It's just Max, I think. It's so comforting to say this. It's just Max, my friend; someone who has no intention of hurting me and truly wants to spend time with and get to know me in a non-abusive way. "It's just Max," and I am safe.

I continue to repeat that phrase every time I feel myself beginning to panic and wanting to run away. For the rest of the conference, I meet Max and we talk until 3 a.m. We pretend to casually run into each other, or even ask the other if they want to meet for lunch and dinner. Max writes me a letter saying, "Look, we have a lot to complain about. We should just eat lunch and dinner together every day." And we do.

I decide I am going to kiss Max. It is the night before our last day at the conference and Max and I are talking and walking around the conference grounds. We reach the edge of the path and look into the woods as the moon hits the leaves. I want to hold his hand. But I don't.

Okay, one more lap, then I'll kiss him, I think as we continue to walk around the same path. *Okay, after this tree, I'll kiss him,* I plan. But I don't. We finally call it a night and walk back toward the entrance of the building. I want to turn and gently kiss him. But I don't.

I get back to my room and I decide to make a plan. First, I am going to write him one final letter – a little sarcastic, of course, but also more serious this time. I am going to tell him how I feel. Even more, I am going to give him the letter, tell him how I feel, then kiss him.

I don't sleep that night. I write his letter and spend the rest of the night imagining our kiss. The next morning, I wake up and immediately start getting ready for the day. As I shower, I replay my plan over and over and over and over and over again in my head. Step by step, everything is accounted for and it is going to be perfect. The butterflies explode in my stomach.

It's the last day of the conference and we are required to dress in professional formal attire, and I am beyond ecstatic for my outfit. I wear a black button up shirt with a tan pencil skirt, black heels, my hair down and wavy with just the right amount of subtle mascara and eyelash curling. I look good and I can't wait for him to see me. I am late for breakfast because I want to make him wait a little. I want to walk through the doorway and feel him slowly look up in awe at me. And he does. But I am too nervous to talk to him, so I ignore him until breakfast is over. As we walk towards each other, I flirtatiously lean back to look him over and proclaim, "Well, look at you. Not too bad at all." We both smile nervously and join the group upstairs. The concluding ceremony is a series of pictures with people I don't really know, acknowledgments, speeches, etc. Through it all, I never forgot the plan. After the final speeches are given, it is time for lunch, and time for the plan.

The Plan

When not too many people are around, sexily walk up to Max and casually say, "Hey, Max, I'm going to check my email really quick. Want to come with me to the computer room?" He will say *yes*, and we will begin our stroll to the computer room. During the walk, we will exchange pleasantries and joke about the previous ceremony we had to endure. I will lead him down the hallway but somehow Max will end up in front of me as we walk into the computer room. *Damn it, no, that won't work.* Fine, I'll be in front the entire way, and when we get into the computer room, I'll just turn around. *Yeah, that will work.* I'll turn around and, before Max can say anything, I will turn and gently kiss him the way all the sexually confident women in movies do. I'll seductively kiss him, slowly grazing his bottom lip with my bottom lip. Then, while looking into his eyes, I'll slip my letter into his pocket and say, "A little something for you to read later." I'll pause for just a second with my hand on his chest, just above his suit jacket pocket, then I'll grin as I walk away, leaving him unbreakably smitten.

What Actually Happened

The room where we are eating lunch is surprisingly vacant. As I enter, I see Max surveying the tables full of boxed lunches. I take a very deep breath and walk toward him. In what feels like seconds, I am standing next to him.

"Max," I say abruptly.

He momentarily postpones his internal debate of ham versus roast beef to say, "Hey." I freeze for a moment before continuing with the plan.

"I'm going to check my email really quick. Want to come with me?" I ask.

"Uh, no, that's okay," he says as he picks up a ham box.

What?! I scream, but only in my head. *What about the plan?* I panic. *Okay, stay calm,* I say to myself.

"Okay, fine," I say. I stand in silence as I pretend to choose between two sandwiches. "Max, can you please just come to the computer room with me? I want to give you a letter." I say.

His eyes move from the sandwich boxes to me, but he doesn't look at me the way I imagined he would.

"Okay," he says.

The walk down the hallway is excruciating. Neither one of us speak, and I can feel his nervous disconnectedness hurling itself around the hallway as we walk. Finally, after what could not have been anything less than a three day walk, we are here, in the computer room. I enter first, and when I turn around, there he is. He is standing there, looking at me. Actually, he is nervously guarded and looking right at me.

Kiss him? I ask in my head. I move closer. *No, he's not moving towards me.* I freeze. *Should I move closer?* I think. *I don't know, I've never done this before,* I panic. *You can't do it now. You've been standing here for way too long,* I conclude. I am paralyzed. He gives me that look again—the look that definitely says that we don't know each other as well as I thought we did, and now he's weirded out. I can feel the plan melting like hot lava. In fact, I kind of wish there was hot lava. Being sucked into a volcano would feel like a wonderful escape right about now.

I panic and blurt out, "I thought we could kiss."

"Oh," Max responds. We both stand awkwardly for a few moments before he places his hands on my hips, pulls me closer, and then our faces and lips touch for approximately half a second. My first kiss.

I hand him the letter and say, "Here, I wrote this for you."

He says, "Okay," takes the letter, and we walk swiftly back down the hallway. The walk back is even more unbearable than the walk to the computer room, and that is it.

We wait together in the same room for a very uncomfortable hour before our rides pick us up. As soon as I get into my friends car, I burst into tears and don't stop crying for about four days. I felt so exposed that I wanted to rip my skin off and hide in someone else's until I felt forgotten.

It wasn't that I was sad or in love or even really that hurt by Max. This journey with Max was my first experience with being vulnerable, with opening myself up just a little and connecting with someone else. It was my first experience with not only wanting to kiss someone but actually kissing him, and the entire experience unleashed a fire hydrant of fears, triggers, bullshit thoughts, wounds, and emotions that I had spent years either suppressing or never even knowing existed.

All the shame, embarrassment, pain, fear, insecurity, vulnerability, violation I had experienced during the abuse ripped open while navigating my connection with Max. I had never felt so exposed in my adult life.

After about a week of trigger-crying and listening to Sheryl Crow's "Strong Enough" on repeat, it hit me: *Holy shit. I can do it.* I realized. *I can do it!*

I felt liberated. For the very first time in my entire life, I connected with a guy. I connected with someone and felt all the feelings that come with that type of connection - both scary and wonderful. *I kissed someone!* I think. *I freaking kissed someone!* After an entire lifetime of believing that I was incapable of simply connecting with someone, let alone kissing them, I did it. I was beginning to understand what a relationship could be (minus the awkward kiss and rejection). I now knew that a relationship was possible for me—that I could not only want to be in one, but I was also capable of actually being in one. My journey with Max taught me one of the most important lessons I've learned in regards to relationships: I can do it. I did do it. And when I'm ready, I'll do it again.

Jackie

Before I continue, I want to discuss why this section was challenging for me to write. My goal for this book is that you read the pages, feel empowered, and rediscover aspects of love that you thought were lost after experiencing abuse. I want to fill you with confidence and self-love so that you know, without a doubt, that no one has the right to take advantage of you. However, I also want to be honest with you and include the stories that are difficult for me to include. That's why I struggled with this section. In order to explain, I have to start where the story ends - when I had sex with Jackie.

After months of beings friends, I decided that I wanted to have sex with Jackie. I also decided that a few drinks could definitely help me feel more comfortable with having sex with Jackie. However, by the end of the night, I was hunched over a wastebasket, trying not to puke, when Jackie made her move. We had sex and, yes, I had initially consented. However, the fact that Jackie felt it was okay to initiate sex while I could barely sit up straight is a violation. She's not a friend, she's not someone who cared about me. She's someone who took advantage of me and violated my trust.

I am including this story because it is an important part of the growth that I've experienced in my life. However, my hesitancy to include this story lays in the fact that I don't want you to read this section and think that I believe that what Jackie did is acceptable, and I especially do not want you to think that I condone anyone initiating sex with someone who is not completely coherent. People who love you and cherish your trust, love, and safety will never have sex with you while you're intoxicated, even if you've consented to sex previously. With that said, here's my story.

For a long time, I accepted the fact that I struggled with being intimate with men, and I accepted the belief that I would never be in a relationship. However, as I got older, I started to notice a growing desire to know what it was like to hold someone's hand, or makeout, or watch a movie and cuddle with someone I felt absolutely safe with and loved by. I knew that being intimate with a man wasn't something I was ready to do yet, but I wondered if I would feel comfortable being intimate with a woman. I was friends with women my whole life. I was able to be myself around my female friends and I felt safe and comfortable and valued while with them—all things I consider to be essential when being intimate with someone. So, I thought that maybe I was meant to be with a woman. A few months later, I met Jackie.

For every positive quality I say about Jackie, I can provide an equally negative quality as well. There were two sides of Jackie. She was welcoming, adventurous, and fun. She was also manipulative and selfish and lied to everyone.

Jackie loved porn, BDSM, making films, photography, and women. She was loud, friendly, manipulative, uninhibited, and on probation for getting into a bar fight, again. Jackie was one of those people who just seemed to attract adventure. She could go to the grocery store to pick up milk and she'd end up with six new friends in the backyard of their mansion while the mascot for the local baseball team shot hotdogs out of a canon for the barbecue party.

I met Jackie at the end of my sophomore year of college. Jackie was twenty-nine and I was nineteen. I quickly realized that hanging out with Jackie usually guaranteed an adventure-filled time. I remember riding on top of her pick-up truck with a camera in my hand as she drove to the top of a hill to document a spiritual wellbeing center. I spent the next two hours learning about healing crystals and auras.

We quickly became friends, and for the rest of the summer I spent almost every day finding something to do with Jackie. We went to the movies, I borrowed her truck, hosted bonfires, and we planned parties at her cabin, during which I helped her demonstrate to everyone how to unhook a bra in less than two seconds.

Jackie was very flirtatious. But she was flirtatious with everyone so, for the majority of our friendship, I didn't think twice about her comments. Honestly, the comments made me feel sexy and desired, and for the first time, feeling sexy and desired didn't totally intimidate me. During a bonfire party at her cabin, Jackie grabbed me, pulled me in close, and danced with me. That was the first time I was ever held by anyone. For a brief second, I felt close and wanted and calm.

That night, all eight of us in the group had to split three rooms. I bunked with Jackie. As we lay in bed, I thought about what it would be like to be intimate with Jackie.

I wake up as I feel Jackie moving around in the bed. A few seconds later, Jackie moves closer and gently pulls me toward her by my hips. She slowly starts massaging my hips and back. It feels good. Maybe I like women. I imagine turning around and kissing her, but I don't do it. I feel her hand move down my thigh and between my legs and that's when I panic, push her hand away, and pretend to wake her up, "Jackie, wake up. You're dreaming and think I'm someone else." She pretends to groggily roll over and I quickly return to my side of the bed.

I am so overwhelmed by feelings of shame and fear of ridicule that I can't sleep for the rest of the night. Early in the morning, I finally get up because I can't take it anymore. I decide to take a shower. I wasn't even intimate with Jackie but I am still standing in the shower, trying not to cry as I desperately attempt to wash off the shame.

Eventually, the rest of the group wakes up and I am just waiting for Jackie to tell everyone how easy it was to almost have sex with me, to tell them how much she knew I wanted it, to tell them how easy it will be to get me next time. I feel like a naive slut and I am waiting to be called one.

That night was my first experience with feeling mortified by intimacy. I didn't even have sex with Jackie and I still felt dirty. It wasn't even the idea of having sex that made me feel ashamed. It was idea of being turned on - by wanting sex - that made me feel terrible. Simply thinking about being intimate with Jackie triggered every feeling of shame that I experienced during the abuse. During the abuse, I was sweaty and sometimes vaginally wet, which made me feel absolutely disgusting. It made me feel dirty. I was told that I was a "dirty slut who wanted it." Jackie was the first time I allowed myself to be turned on in the presence of another person. Naturally, it triggered a lot of wounds from my past.

Jackie didn't tell anyone about that night and she never ridiculed or embarrassed me. A few weeks passed and, although I hadn't completely worked through all the emotions from that night, I decided that I wanted to try to be intimate with Jackie. I knew that we weren't in love. I knew that Jackie was in an open relationship with someone else. I knew that, if we were to have sex, I would be using Jackie to test whether or not I could be intimate with someone and Jackie would be using me for sex. But I also knew that I was comfortable with her, at least more sexually comfortable than I had been with other people.

We decided to go to a bar. I was too young to be legally allowed in a bar but Jackie's friend owned a club downtown and was going to let me in. I put on my best adult-looking club-like outfit - a pencil skirt and blouse - which did nothing except highlight the fact that I was underage and had never been in a club before. Jackie's friend who owned the bar gave us free drinks all night. The more I drank, the less nervous I became.

"What would you do to me?" I ask with a grin.

"What?" Jackie asks, surprised.

"If we had sex, what would you do?"

Jackie, turns to look at me. I have her attention. "Well..." she starts to answer. Jackie continues to describe a possible sexual experience. Her description isn't as detailed as I hoped. For as bold as she is, the question seems to catch her off guard.

About three hours and nine drinks later, Jackie calls a friend to pick us up and we are back at her house. We stumble up to her room and onto her bed.

"Ugh! I'm going to puke," I say as I demand that Jackie bring the trash bin from the bathroom into the bedroom. I sit with the trash bin in my lap as Jackie puts a movie on.

"What is this?" I drunkenly ask.

"It's a movie," Jackie replies.

I ignore her response and continue to stare into the bottom of the trash bin as my chin rests on its rim. Then I hear the moans. Jackie's movie is actually a full-length pornography with surprisingly impressive special effects.

"Are we watching a-" but my thoughts are broken by a very urgent desire to hurl. "Ugh! I want to puke!" I yell.

Jackie's tone softens, "Okay, calm down. It's okay." Jackie moves behind me and starts massaging my back. After a few minutes, she moves from my back and starts rubbing my stomach. I am actually surprised when my stomach starts to feel better. After about ten minutes of that, my desire to puke has subsided. I put the trash bin back in the bathroom and walk back to the room.

"Okay, what the hell are we watching?" I ask as I sit back down on the bed.

"It's porn," Jackie replies. "There's lesbian sex, but don't worry, you can close your eyes during those parts because I know you're straight."

I roll my eyes and continue to watch as swashbuckling porn stars sword fight with skeletons then have sex. Jackie moves from her spot next to me back to the position behind me. She pulls me in and begins massaging my back. After a few minutes, we are having sex.

I wake up the next morning and I feel sexy as I notice the sun shining in through the window onto my shoulders and back. I hear Jackie stir a bit as she moves closer then falls back asleep. I've only ever experienced "the morning after reactions" in movies. The characters either turn towards each other in the morning sun and smile lovingly as they kiss each other, managing to ignore morning breath. Or one half of the one-night stand leaves, emotionally detached and sexually satisfied, while the other watches from bed and tries to hide the fact that they feel used, sad, and have morning breath. Based on those movie scenarios, I thought that I only had those two options to choose from. Jackie and I aren't in love so that rules out the first option, which leaves the second option of feeling used and uncomfortable. But I don't feel used. I do feel a little detached, but not in a mean way – more in a calm way, as if to say, "Okay, I did that and I'm still okay." I realize I have more options to choose from than just the two that I've gleaned from b-list romantic comedies.

This could feel really good with someone I care about, I think. It's at this moment that I realize that I can be intimate with someone. I can find someone who I really care about, who really cares about me. We can be intimate and it can feel really good.

I get up and leave the room while Jackie is still sleeping. I'm not going to run away, but I want to be alone. I don't have any clean clothes, so I put on the pencil skirt and blouse from the night before and go outside. There is a maelstrom of triggers and fears that could be careening through my head, but I am surprisingly calm. Yes, it is going to be awkward when Jackie finally wakes up. Yes, maybe this was crazy. Yes, maybe this could make a hilarious story later on. Yes, I feel weird, uncomfortable, excited, afraid, happy, depressed, but I was intimate with someone and I don't care about anything else at that moment. I did it! I did it and I know that I am okay.

I walk back into the house and see Jackie coming down the stairs. I freeze. I'm not sure what to say.

"Morning," I blurt out.

"Good morning," Jackie replies, then she continues. "You hurt my wrist last night."

While we were at the bar that night, we drunkenly decided to arm wrestle and I guess I had accidentally hurt her wrist. But I am too anxious to move on with the day to really hear her so I continue without acknowledging her comment.

"Let's get some breakfast," I reply as I walk to the kitchen.

Jackie follows.

"You really hurt my wrist," Jackie says again as she rubs her arm.

"Okay," I say as I grab a cereal box.

"Seriously, you really hurt it and you haven't even said sorry," she says, hurt.

I look up, surprised. "What?" I gently ask.

"I've told you like three times how you hurt my wrist and you haven't said sorry once," she replies.

I can hear that she is hurt. She feels used. "I... I'm sorry," I stumble. I am taken aback. I was so focused on shielding myself from the possibility of being hurt by Jackie that I completely dismissed the idea that I could possibly hurt her.

Until that moment, I never knew that I could hurt someone I had sex with. I truly beleived that the minute I had sex with someone, all of my power was gone. I believed that I needed to guard myself from meanness and ridicule. Of course, I did not want to hurt anyone, and the thought of hurting Jackie made me sad. But realizing that I was capable of hurting someone meant that I was an equal participant in the emotional and physical act of sex. Up until that moment, I had assumed and accepted that sex meant that I became a passive object to be used. I thought that having sex would either hurt because I would have to do it when I didn't really want to, or it would hurt because the individual I had sex with would be abusive afterwards. When I realized that I hurt Jackie, I realized that sex is not an unemotional act where one individual acts as an object from which the other can steal everything. Both people are vulnerable during sex and they want their partners to be nice to them afterwards. I realized that sex is supposed to be nice, not hurtful. Most importantly, I realized that I am a participant in sex, not someone sex is happening to. I decided that the next time I participated in sex, it would be with someone really special and that it would feel really great.

Long-Term Relationships

It's a Monday night in February and, after a disappointing outcome to what I thought was going to be a successful connection with someone, I am frustrated. I throw up my arms and assertively say, "Universe! I'm ready!"

I hesitate for a second and rephrase my statement, "...I think I'm ready." I think for another second, then ask, "Am I ready?"

"You're ready to try," I hear in response.

I smile, nod my head and say, "I'm ready to try."

That Friday night, four days after my declaration of readiness for a relationship, I meet Ben.

Ben

I just turned twenty-one and I have decided that my fear of intimacy is no longer greater than my desire to connect with someone the way I know I can. No, I haven't experienced the type of intimacy and closeness with someone that I feel is ideal, but I have experienced multiple attempts at intimacy and I now know being intimate is possible.

I am a little bitter about having met someone last week and then never hearing from him again, so I'm not really on the lookout for a love connection. Instead, I want to wear my flannel shirt and cowgirl boots, head to the country bar near my university, and disregard men as I dance the night away. My plan to disregard men for the night is short-lived soon after I walk into the bar.

As I walk to the restroom with one of my girlfriends, I am suddenly bombarded by the most intense feeling of being admired I have ever experienced. I think, *Holy crap! Who is this coming from? It's going to be a good night tonight!* After I return from the restroom and meet back with my friends, I quickly sense the same vibe. I look around the bar until I see him, Ben that is, at the other side of the bar, looking at me while his friends continue to talk around him. But Ben and I don't talk until about two hours later. Actually, the conversation begins while Ben is away in the restroom and one of his friends comes over to talk to me.

"Hey, my friend really likes you," this guy says to me.

"Is he the one who's been checking me out all night, but won't talk to me?" I quip back.

Taken aback, his friend slowly nods his head. I continue, "Well, you can tell him that if he wants to talk to me, he can come over here and talk to me."

Ben returns from the bathroom and before he can be entirely caught up on his friend's matchmaking tactics, another of his friends comes up to me and says, "Hi, you seem really nice and my friend really wants to dance with you."

I playfully reply, "Well, tell him to come over here and ask me!" By then, Ben looks mortified by his friends' interventions and hesitantly walks over.

"Would you like to dance?" he asks me.

"I like to lead," I say as I grin.

Ben drops my hand, spins around as if I am guiding him, and says, "Lead me!"

At that moment, I decide to try. I spend the rest of the night dancing and getting to know Ben. The first few tidbits of critical information that we learn about each other is that we share a mutual love for baseball, Ben and Jerry's ice cream, and the movie The Godfather.

At the end of the night, I get ready to leave with my friends, Ben runs to catch up with me and asks for my phone number. I give it to him, but not before saying, "I don't respond to anyone who waits more than a day to contact me."

"Okay," he says confidently. I smile and walk away.

Less than five minutes later, Ben texts me to ask, "Is this too soon to text?"

I spend the next three weekends coming up with excuses for me and my friends to return to the country line dancing bar they kind of hate so that I can meet up with Ben, but pretend like I'm not excited to. As Ben jokingly says, I spend the next several months "putting him through the ringer." It's not that I didn't like Ben. In fact, it was the opposite. Ben was the first man I felt ready to enter into a relationship with. When Ben gave me three feet, I gave him an inch and then pushed him away for the rest of the two feet and eleven inches. Again, it's not that I didn't want him to stay. I just wanted to make sure that he would stay. If he kept coming back after so many months of being pushed away, maybe he'd stay when I finally let him. And, most importantly, maybe he'd stay when I tell him that I experienced abuse, that I struggle with intimacy, and that it's going to take time for me to be able to hold his hand, to connect while I'm having sex, to learn to love him.

A few weeks after seeing each other, I decide that I wanted to give Ben a blow job and allow him to go down on me. It is official. I am going to give and receive oral. I am terrified. I have read every stupid article in magazines about how to give "mind-blowingly mind-blowing blow jobs," *but do I really know how to do it?* I decide to meet with one of my friends who I know has experience in the matter.

During the meeting, after fielding a series of questions about techniques and positions, she says to me, "It's not about doing it because you think you have to. It's about wanting to make your partner feel good." Remember my bullshit thought that "being sexual is the only way I have power?" Until this moment, I viewed oral sex – and any sex-related activity – as something that I had to be good at in order to protect myself. If I couldn't give a good blow job then I would have to admit that I had never given a blow job before, and if I admitted that then I would have to talk about how freaking intimidated I was by intimacy, and then I would have to get into more detail about the abuse, and then he would, for sure, view me as totally messed up by the abuse. He would view me as a wounded little girl who had nothing to offer him sexually and all of my power would be lost. He would hurt me and leave. Sex, as a way of expressing my love, making my partner feel valued, and as a way of connecting instead of a means of demonstrating my worth, proving my value, and convincing my partner to stay was something that never crossed my mind before. I didn't learn any new oral tricks that day, but I did receive the best sex tip I would ever learn.

Ben and I are together for six years before deciding to end the relationship. It isn't that he is a bad person or that I am a bad person. Our relationship needs to end because we came into each other's lives at a specific time, for a specific reason. After six years, we no longer need each other for the same reasons. We outgrew each other. We've been trying to force each other back into the roles we played at the beginning of our relationship and it's hurting both of us.

Was the love we shared deep, conscious love? No. We spent most of our relationship attempting to fill our voids through the other. Despite the fact that our relationship wasn't perfect, we both gave the best love we were capable of at the time. Through my journey with Ben, I learned how to let someone in. I learned that loving someone meant sharing things with my partner that I never told anyone—and trusting him with that information. I learned that love is a choice, it's something you choose to do everyday, even when it's difficult or you don't feel like doing it. I learned what it feels like to have someone want to protect me and even take care of me—and I learned how to let someone do that for me.

Through Ben's family, I learned what a family was and I developed a deeper sense of what I want my own family to be like in the future. I learned lessons as simple as discovering what it felt like to be held, and as complex as learning how to work through a trigger with my partner during sex. Despite the fact that the relationship ended and, at the time, that ending felt like it would be the end of my heart, my journey with Ben was a beautiful first experience with love, and it laid the foundation of what I do and do not want for future relationships.

Steve

Steve and I have been dating for a little over a year. I'm fast asleep and dreaming that Steve and I are sitting on a couch, talking with a therapist.

"Katie, Steve is no longer your boyfriend," says the therapist in my dream. "He's your dad now."

I look at Steve, shrug my shoulders and respond, "Okay, I'm fine with that."

I met Steve through mutual friends a week after Ben and I broke up. To say that I was an emotional wreck and in no way ready for another relationship is an understatement. But the voids I was experiencing felt so unbearable that I jumped right into a relationship with Steve.

Steve was one of the nicest men I ever met. Although he looked like an NFL linebacker, he wouldn't hurt a fly. Steve was lighthearted, gentle, communicative. He could easily share his innermost feelings, and deeply listened when I expressed mine. The only downside of the relationship was that we were almost never physically intimate. Steve was entirely disinterested in sex. And although this eventually became a huge problem in our relationship, for a long time, I was completely okay with not having sex. I was being held, taken care of, bought dinner, listened to, protected, all without having any sexual intimacy at all—it was the perfect paternal relationship. Let me say that again. It was the perfect paternal relationship.

When I had that dream, I realized I was dating my dad. No, I wasn't dating someone like Tim, instead I was dating the dad I always wanted but never had.

My journey with Steve helped me realize how essential it was that I take a serious look at my voids, my wounds, my inner children, and start doing some inner work on my own.

The Dating Hiatus

I am sitting on my couch, alone in my apartment. I am calm right now, but I can feel the excruciating pain I've grown accustomed to over the past few weeks waiting below the surface. "Lean in," I say out loud. "Lean in and get cozy with your voids."

All I want to do is go to the bar with my friends and get hit on. I know it's meaningless. I know it won't heal anything, but, damn it, maybe it will make me feel better for just a second. But I refuse. None of this is who I am. I am an independent, strong-willed, badass woman who has never needed a man, but I am spiraling in love addiction and withdrawal. I know that the only way out is some serious healing

When we are in love, several euphoria-inducing chemicals, such as adrenaline, oxytocin, and dopamine are released in the brain. The same sensations are triggered when we do cocaine. Meaning, love is just as addictive as cocaine. When we lose love, we go through withdrawal very similar to the way we would if we were addicted to drugs: sleeplessness, loss of appetite, not being able to think about anything but the person (drug) we can't have, trying to get our fix through anything we possibly can.

I jumped into a relationship with Steve immediately after breaking up with Ben as a way to soothe my love withdrawal. When Steve and I broke up, I was thrown right back into my withdrawl symptoms. I needed a fix. So I signed up for dating apps. I quickly met a guy who I dated for a few weeks, all while starting to talk with Ben again. I was an emotional ping pong ball bouncing aimlessly from one void-filling guy to the next. At the height of my addiction, I slept with both the guy I met on the dating app and Ben, back and forth for a week. By the end of the week, I felt empty, used, and alone with every one of my gaping voids I had spent the past seven years avoiding through relationships. After hitting what felt like an emotional rock bottom in regards to relationships, I decided to go cold turkey.

"I am going on a six month dating hiatus," I proclaim. "No dates, no dating apps, no flirting, no talking with exes. You're not even allowed to look at guys right now," I tell myself sternly.

For the next six months, I date myself. I get to know myself again. What do I like to do? What style of clothing do I like to wear now? What are my career goals and how do I plan to achieve them? What do I like sexually? Do I want to get married and have kids? What type of love do I want to give and receive from the people in my life? What are the deepest, darkest parts of myself that I've been hiding from? How can I heal and love those parts of myself? Do I like sushi?

I work on healing my voids with self-love, tending to my wounds from the past, and deep-diving into who I truly am. Is it easy? Hell no. There are times when I feel like I am going to drown in my own emotions. There is so much crying and watching *This Is Us* reruns and crying more. But there are also beautiful, empowering moments between the tears.

I get new clothes that I feel finally reflect my style. I discover a passion for jiu-jitsu. I go on adventures, learn to ride a bike, try new restaurants, laugh, meet new friends, deepen my relationships with current friends, quit my job and launch my own business, start the process of publishing my book, and discover that I do, in fact, like sushi. My dating hiatus holds some of the most life-changing months of life. I will recommend a dating hiatus to everyone I meet for the rest of my life. In fact, before my last breath, I will look around the room and whisper wisely, "Go on a dating hiatus," and I hope all of them listen because I am old and wise and dead now.

When I was finally ready to begin dating again, I was doing so as a whole person. For the first time in my life, I truly knew who I was. I knew what I believed in. I knew what I wanted for my life. I knew what I wanted and needed from a partner. I understood my old dating patterns, the fear they were based in, and how they affected the partners I had previously chosen to date. Here are a few of the things I learned:

I was Codependent

There was a time when Ben helped pay my bills so that I could quit my job and pursue my dreams. That was beautiful and, if I were in a healed space, I probably would have been able to fully dive in and make some dreams come true. But I was frozen. We had been together for about four years and I knew our relationship was ending. The closer we both came to realizing that our relationship wasn't working, the more each of my ignored and unhealed wounds hurt. The place I had hidden all of my wounds, behind my relationship with Ben, was starting to fall apart. I became completely dependent on Ben financially and I felt like I was suffocating. I was ignoring every part of myself that was screaming, "You're unhappy in this relationship!" I was ignoring every part of myself that was screaming, "Ben is unhappy in this relationship!" Instead, I curled up in a metaphorical ball, closed my eyes, and squeezed as hard as I could in hopes that I would vanish into an abyss of relationship safety and "love."

I was actually trying to make money. But no matter how hard I tried, I could not make enough money to pay all my bills. Then, one day, it hit me: *I won't let myself make money because, if I do, there won't be anything forcing me and Ben to stay together and I know I will leave.* The truth was, I wanted to leave. I wanted to make money, move out, get my own place, start a new life, and really start living my dreams. I also knew that if I did that, my relationship with Ben would be over. Ben had been my sole source of safety for years, and I knew that once I allowed myself to start making money and was no longer dependent on him, I wouldn't be able to ignore the fact that I was unhappy. I would leave, we would break up, and that safety would be gone. Two months after I came to that realization, I had a well-paying job, I found an apartment, and Ben and I broke up.

Codependency can be subtle, and it manifests in relationships in a variety of ways. Trauma led me to believe that it was not safe to trust or rely on anyone. Because of this, the world seemed terrifying to me. Ben became the one person in the world who I truly allowed myself to trust and feel safe with. Without him, I felt completely alone and exposed. For this reason, I subconsciously developed ways to keep our relationship intact. I made myself completely dependent on him so that I couldn't choose to leave and he couldn't abandon me. That's codependency.

When we experience trauma, we are often physically or psychologically abandoned. As a result, we subconsciously develop ways to protect ourselves from being abandoned again. Many times, this involves either choosing partners who are dependent on us or becoming dependent ourselves. Some people are drawn to partners with addictions or mental illnesses because these partners "need" them. Some people choose to believe that they cannot leave a relationship they are unhappy in because they have "responsibilities" to people who are dependent on them. Other people find ways to become dependent so that the people they love can't abandon them. All of these scenarios are just masked codependency.

I encourage you to be very real with yourself. Are there codependent patterns in your relationships? The purpose of this practice is not to judge yourself. You've been through enough already, you don't need to beat yourself up over this. Simply witness your patterns, love yourself through them, and then move forward with the rest of the activities in this chapter.

My Fear of Abandonment Sabotaged Everything

Most relationship issues can be broken down into two categories: the fear of abandonment and the fear of engulfment. The fear of abandonment is the fear of losing love. Fear of engulfment is the fear of being suffocated, controlled, or trapped by love. Both fears usually develop as a result of trauma and years of experiencing unhealthy love. Many of us are actually afraid of both and can fluctuate between the two.

A perfect example of the fear of engulfment is my journey with Kenny. I pushed him away and cut him off completely because I was terrified that his love meant that I would have to be physically intimate when I didn't want to.

The fear of abandonment can be seen in all of my long-term relationships. I only ever dated the men who pursued me most adamantly. I didn't care if I was attracted to them, or if our personalities were compatible, or if our senses of humor were aligned. All I cared about was how intensely they wanted to date me. If they pursued me more intensely and for longer than any of the other guys, then I dated him. I was afraid of being abandoned again. I believed that a relentless pursuit meant that he would stay.

I Was Addicted to Unavailable Men

I spent my entire childhood chasing the affections of Lisa and Tim. I tried being quiet, never speaking in hopes that I would be rewarded for my good behavior. I made myself small, hoping that being humble could gain their affection. When that didn't work, I tried humor in hopes that making them laugh would gain their approval. I shifted identities constantly in order to try to become a version of myself that they could love. As a result, I learned that love is an elusive thing that I must relentlessly chase.

As an adult, this manifested as chasing emotionally unavailable men—men who weren't capable of expressing or allowing themselves to receive love. That was my comfort zone. Every time I met one of these men, without realizing it, something deep down inside of me was triggered. This fierce competitive drive of needing to find a way to make a person love me exploded out of me and I ended up chasing another emotionally incapable version of Lisa or Tim. I became addicted to the chase. I became addicted to making this person love me. It was as if a part of me thought, *Well, I couldn't get Lisa or Tim to love me, but if I can get this emotionally inept person to love me, then I win! I win! I will finally have proof that Lisa and Tim's lack of love had nothing to do with me because this person is just as emotionally unavailable as they were but he fell in love with me. I win and Lisa and Tim were wrong!* The thing is, Lisa and Tim were wrong, and I don't need to gain the love of anyone to prove that.

The thing about emotionally unavailable people is that they are just that, unavailable. As painful as it may be to accept, there is absolutely nothing you will ever do to open their ability to love and receive love—and this has nothing to do with you and everything to do with their own unhealed wounds.

I Learned to Accept the Bare Minimum

As I stated before, I spent my entire childhood doing everything I could possibly think of to try and gain the affection of Lisa and Tim. When I did receive the slightest (and I mean absolute slightest) demonstration of affection, I felt like I won an Olympic gold medal. I earned their love, that was all I needed. That itty bitty, bare minimum demonstration of kindness was enough love to fill me up. As a result, I learned to accept the bare minimum.

I learned to ration the affection I did receive as if it were the last chocolate bar and I was stuck on a deserted island. As an adult, this manifested as accepting half-ass efforts from partners. I accepted it when a partner didn't call when he said he would because, when we were together, he seemed like he cared. "I thought about buying you flowers today," he would say, and I thought that was good enough. He thought about it, he didn't actually put forth the effort or time or money to do it, but he thought about it and that was enough for me. He forgot my birthday but felt bad when he remembered, that was enough. I was constantly accepting nothing, so I attracted partners who wanted to give me just that.

By the end of my dating hiatus (and years of self-work leading up to that hiatus), I was hella self-aware. I became an expert in identifying my wounds and analyzing how those wounds were contributing to my unhealthy relationship patterns. I became a professional at identifying the types of men I was attracted to because of what I learned to believe about love. This awareness helped me rapidly identify red flags, leave unhealthy relationships, and identify unhealthy love from miles away. But all of that self-awareness and consciousness that allowed me to identify healthy love didn't change the fact that I was still had no idea what healthy love looked like or felt like. It wasn't enough to know how to identify unhealthy love. I needed to learn what healthy love was. Here's where I started:

How to Learn What Healthy Love Is
Know Your Wounded Areas

Unhealed wounds will affect every part of our lives. That said, there is something about relationships that can unveil wounds tenfold. Romantic relationships seem to be the area when our wounds feel most raw. For this reason, they also tend to be where they sabotage our growth most. What wounds felt most raw? How did those wounds lead to hurtful or unhealthy actions? Maybe you have a fear of abandonment and it caused you to cling to an unhealthy relationship for way too long. Maybe you had controlling, abusive parents so you learned that love is manipulative and painful, so you pushed away your last healthy-love partner. Take some time to reflect on your past relationships, the wounds that were exposed during the relationships, and the ways you may have acted out as a result.

Learn What Healthy *Love* Looks Like

Surround yourself with videos, books, movies, articles, and real-life relationships that are healthy. I did not have one example of healthy love that I could pull from my past, so how the hell could I know what to look for in real life? I couldn't. I had to learn what healthy love looked like. I started paying attention to the couples in my life whose love I admired—I noticed the way my friend would gently touch the back of her boyfriend's neck when he walked into the room. I noticed the way they acknowledged that the other was important simply by making eye contact even when things were really busy. I noticed the way they laughed together, the way they handled conflict together, the way they planned together. When I couldn't be with real-life couples, I read about healthy love. I watched movies and videos. I did everything I could to rewire my brain from accepting unhealthy love as the norm and learning to recognize and expect healthy love.

Pull From Your Other *Relationships*

The Universe has blessed me with a group of friends who have become my family. I know, without a doubt, they will be there when I need them to be. I know this because they are also there when I don't need them to be. The love we share exists during all circumstances, easy and challenging. The support and love I receive from them is given with no strings or expectations attached, and I return that love in the same fashion. You may not be able to pull examples of healthy love from your previous romantic relationships, but there are other relationships in your life where true love is present. Pull from those experiences.

Know What Healthy *Love* Feels Like

Our feelings are the number one influencer of our thoughts and actions, whether we like it or not. If all we have ever felt is unhealthy love, that is all we will ever see in our lives because that is all we know how to recognize. We must feel healthy love in order to find it. If you're like I was, you may not have any examples of healthy love to remember feeling. That's okay. You have to imagine what healthy love feels like. And I don't mean sit and think about it for a little bit. I mean freaking deep dive into what it feels like to experience healthy love. Feel, in the depths of your soul, what it feels like to be truly loved.

If you're struggling to get started, start small.

I imagine how it feels when my partner goes shopping with me, even though he knows it will be boring but he simply wants to spend time with me. I imagine what it feels like when I say, "I'm really thirsty," and he gets up and grabs me water. I imagine what it feels like when he remembers and asks about an important work event that I talked about last week. I imagine what it feels like when my partner cheers me on for an accomplishment. I imagine cooking dinner together on a Friday night.

All of these examples are simple, right? Moment of honesty: when I was first doing this healing work and making my list, I believed that these examples were unrealistically high expectations. *Seriously?!* As abuse survivors, we were taught to accept the absolute bare minimum. I'm telling you right now, bare minimum is not healthy love and it's no longer acceptable. So, now that you've made your start-small list, I want you to go bigger.

Imagine that your boyfriend calls and asks to meet you for lunch. When you arrive, he has take-out from your favorite restaurant. He packed wine in a thermos to keep it cool and he brought two wine glasses for you both to drink from. He brought flowers in a vase for you to take with you after lunch. And he wrote you a love letter. Imagine how it feels that he put this much time, energy, and thought into a simple Tuesday afternoon lunch with you. Imagine how much effort he puts into the even bigger parts of your relationship. Imagine what it feels like to receive this love knowing that he wants nothing in return from you but to know that you are happy and feel loved.

This is not a made-up scenario. I actually witnessed this lunch date. I had spent so much time simply hoping a date would be nice enough to pay for my cup of coffee. Now, I was witnessing, in real time, a Hallmark-worthy romantic moment. The best part of it all was that the woman in this situation wasn't even blown away. She was just like,

"Yeah, that's nice, thank you." She didn't feel indebted by his love or unworthy. She just accepted this love as the standard.

At that moment, I said to myself, "Girl, you need to step up your expectations game." I started paying attention to demonstrations of the type of love that I wanted in my life. Witnessing healthy love has a positive domino effect. Once you see that healthy love is possible, you start to allow yourself to imagine how it would feel to experience it. Once you allow yourself to imagine what it would feel to experience it, you allow yourself to want healthy love and you set new standards that allow that type of love to flow into your life easily and constantly.

Stop Playing the Victim and *Forgive* Yourself

"Wow, you did it again," I say as I sit heartbroken in my car, crying after a break-up. "You let someone treat you like shit again," I continue. "You let yourself fall in love with another emotionally unavailable person because you can't get over your own shit." As if that weren't enough, I add, "Are you ready to love yourself? Are you finally going to stop doing this and love yourself?" I berate.

This type of self-talk was damaging on several levels, but two of the most important include: 1.) I was positioning myself as a victim—a victim who has no control over my own actions, and a victim to someone else who hurt me. In doing so, I was trapping myself in the pain and my past. 2.) I was berating myself for opening my heart to someone and sharing my love—the absolute greatest power we have in this lifetime.

Yes, opening your heart to someone makes you vulnerable to having your heart broken, but it also opens you up to the deep, loving relationships you have with your family, friends, and partners. It opens you up to meaningful connections at work, it opens you up to your passions and goals in life. If you aren't capable of opening your heart to people who, yes, may end up hurting you, you will never be open to all the good things in your life either. Loving is not a weakness. It is the greatest gift we are capable of giving and receiving as humans. Never beat yourself up for sharing your love with someone.

You are not a victim. You are a powerful goddess who can heal both herself and others with her love, so start acting like it! Start by apologizing and forgiving yourself.

"Baby girl, I am so sorry that I have been so mean to you about falling in love with this person. You loved him because you know that, like everyone else on this planet, he needed love, and your love is powerful. I am in complete awe of the way you connect with others through your love and I never want you to stop doing that. I'm also sorry for ignoring some of the signs that I saw while dating him. There were moments that indicated he was not emotionally available, but I ignored them because I wanted this to be the right relationship for me. I am sorry for that."

Now, forgive yourself, "I forgive me. And I love me." Boom.

Increase Your Sense of *Entitlement*

Trauma survivors have a diminished sense of entitlement, so it is difficult for us to imagine getting what we want. We've been conditioned to accept the bare minimum so we don't believe that receiving more is a possibility. We end up calibrating our sense of entitlement downward and spending the rest of our lives reluctant to hope for more.

I am focusing on relationships right now, but increasing your sense of entitlement is the best piece of advice I can give you for all aspects of your life. Entitlement has gotten a bad reputation, and rightfully so in the cases where this quality is abused. But entitlement itself is simply knowing that you have the right to live the absolute best life possible. It's knowing what you are putting into the world through your love and effort, and expecting the same amount of love and effort in return. So, increase that sense of entitlement, girl.

- "I expect my partner to call me instead of text."
- "I expect that the partner I choose to date has healed their wounds and is entering into this relationship as a whole person."
- "I expect that my partner sees me – sees all of my parts – and witnesses every part of who I am without judgment or without feeling threatened by my shine."
- "I expect my date to put some goddamn pride in his/her appearance during our first date and not show up looking like he/she just rolled out of bed."

You attract what you accept. If you accept the bare minimum, you will constantly attract partners just waiting to give you nothing. If you believe that you are incapable of healthy love, you will constantly attract partners who validate that belief. If you accept that you never learned what healthy love looks like and believe that you'll never be able to find it, then you're right. Increase your sense of entitlement and expect more from yourself, the world, and your partners.

Call a Meeting With Your Past Selves

"You are an independent, autonomous, badass adult woman in all other aspects of your life," she says, "but you enter into relationships as a little girl."

I called a relationship coach. I was so convinced that there was an unhealed part of myself that I couldn't identify that was sabotaging my relationships that I set up a free consultation call with a relationship coach. She said a lot of things, some were true, some weren't. But when it came to the above statement, she was absolutely right. It was difficult to hear and admit, but it was true. Before that conversation, just the thought of going on a date elicited feelings of raw childlike vulnerability. But I never really thought about why I felt that way. It wasn't until I dove a little deeper that I started hearing my inner little girls, "What if he doesn't like me?" one asks. "He's not going to stay," another begins to panic. "What if he thinks my body is gross?" said my pre-teen self. "I need someone to protect me," one states. "Maybe he will protect me. Make sure he will protect me!" she nervously calls out.

My little girl selves had been leading my romantic interactions for the entirety of my life. It was time that I, my adult woman self, took the lead. So I called a meeting.

"Hey, baby girls," I say as I look around and see my past selves from age six all the way up to just a few years ago. "I want to talk with you about something important," I say.

"I know that our parents weren't very nice and that left a space in our hearts where we wish a mom or a dad could be. And there are times where that space feels so empty that it hurts, and we really want to fill it with someone else," I continue. "We've been putting a lot of men in there because we want a dad, but that hasn't been working. In fact, it actually ends up hurting us more," I say. "But we have all the mom and dad energy we could ever need. We are our moms and our dads and we are supposed to fill those spaces for each other. I am your mom and dad and I am going to love you and protect you for the rest of your life. You never have to worry again."

I pause to look at the years of past selves all gathered around me. I imagine being my mother and looking at me. I am so proud of the woman I am. I am in awe of my beauty, inside and out. I just keep thinking, "I can't believe I made her!" As I imagine this mother energy, I feel loved on a level I haven't experienced before. I feel nurtured and protected and guided. My past selves feel it, too.

Now, I imagine being my dad. I am filled with pride for how incredible I am. I have made every one of my goals come true. I'm also stunned by my beauty. I think, *Does she realize how many men are swooning over her all the time?* I am protective. I know that I am completely capable of taking care of myself and I respect my strength, but I also know that if I ever bring home a man who doesn't appreciate every part of who I am, I will run that man out the door. As I feel this father energy, I feel protected, I feel trusted, I feel secure in knowing that it's safe to expect to receive everything that I want. My past selves feel this, too.

"I am your mom and your dad," I say. "Whenever you need a parent, I am here."

I can feel a void healing.

"Now, you all have been leading the way in my relationships so far. And I am always going to make sure that I include you in my relationship choices," I say, "because you all have deep wisdom that I need." I continue, "But I am going to lead my relationships from now on."

Bryan

"So you have a million questions for me, huh?" I ask as I casually walk toward my car, knowing that he will follow.

"I do. You want to talk about them over dinner sometime?" Bryan asks with the same shockingly over-inflated yet alluring confidence I've been bantering with for the past few months.

I put my bag in my car and turn to look at him. I am interested, but I'm not sure if I want to take the leap.

"I'm not a hook-up person," I say sternly.

"I don't think that at all," he says seriously.

"And I'm not looking to rush into anything," I continue. "Maybe we can hang out as friends."

"I don't want to do that," he says with a directness that tells me he is the type of person who knows what he does and does not want and isn't afraid to be honest about it.

I start laughing. No man has ever responded to my suggestion of being friends in this way. I'm impressed. I no longer want to just be friends either.

"Okay, I have a lot going on for the next few weeks. Ask me again in two weeks," I say with a grin.

"Two weeks," he says nodding as we both smirk and part ways.

I get in my car and pause for a moment. It's been a long time since I've been interested in someone. "If I'm going to do this, I'm doing things differently this time," I say.

For most of my life, I believed that being in a relationship was the worst thing that I could do. The only examples of relationships I had were the one Lisa and Tim had with each other, and the one that they had with my sister and I—all of which taught me to believe that love was directly related to violence, pain, shame, fear, and the feeling of being trapped and controlled. Needless to say, when I got older, I wasn't giddy to jump into a relationship. In fact, for a long time, I went the opposite direction and claimed to be adamantly against relationships. But there was always a part of me that whispered that a different type of love was possible.

I became curious. I wanted to test the waters, but I needed a way to do so without opening myself up to the same type of painful relationship I had experienced in the past. So, in my mind, being vulnerable was not an option. I believed that if I allowed myself to be vulnerable and was hurt again, it would result in the most catastrophic emotional meltdown of my life. In addition to that, I knew that I had lost myself in my previous relationships. I knew that I had made myself small and positioned myself as a victim in order to attract boyfriends who wanted to "protect" me and who could fill my safety void. I had lost myself with these partners while never being fully vulnerable with them. I was afraid that if I was fully vulnerable with a partner, I would lose myself completely. To me, being fully vulnerable wasn't an option. I needed another way.

So, I played games. I played ALL the games. I let him get close to me, then pushed him away. I ignored his calls so that I didn't seem too available. I never initiated a text conversation because I didn't want to look too interested. I flirted with other guys to make him jealous. I constantly looked for ways to ensure that I had just the right amount of power over his emotions so that I never had to risk being truly vulnerable and getting hurt. But it was freaking exhausting. Building walls is an emotional full-time job, and it obviously left no room for any actual connection with a partner who, in the end, I did want to have a relationship with. Not surprisingly, those relationships ended. And it hurt both of us. Not only that, but I always ended up wondering, *If I had been nicer or more open or I hadn't played so many games, would it have lasted? Would the relationship have worked if I had just been myself?*

Behind the surface level games were even deeper games that I played not only with him but also with myself. I was in a competition with myself to ensure that, no matter how much I wanted to connect with this person, I never let myself be influenced by him. I believed that if I let him influence me in any way that I was weakening myself, giving up a part of who I was, and opening myself up to be controlled by him. As I say this out loud, I realize just how irrational it sounds, but for the majority of my life, that belief felt so real. Ben once showed me a way to make fluffier scrambled eggs, but my fear of being influenced was so strong that, even when I was alone in my own kitchen, I refused to implement his scrambled egg making technique. *It's freaking scrambled eggs!* But I honestly believed that this egg recipe would be a descent into a downward spiral of self-abandon and codependency. *Can we all agree now that fear makes us believe stupid shit?*

After my dating hiatus, I feel truly whole and centered in who I am. I know what I want from life and I am making it happen. I also know that everything I previously learned about relationships is untrue. Although my previous relationships ended, through them, I learned that what I experienced as a child was not love. I also discovered the type of relationship that I do want and the type of relationship that is possible. I know that everything I have done in the past is not going to lead to the type of love that I desire. No, I wasn't actively looking to date anoyone, but I can feel that the Universe is pushing me toward a lesson with Bryan, so I decide to give it a try. As I sit in my car, I conclude that I am going to do things differently this time. I'm not playing games. Every time my fear tells me to do something, I am going to do the opposite. I am going to be truly vulnerable.

Fast forward two weeks. Bryan and I are getting coffee.

"I know this is kind of gross," Bryan says as he pulls out his keys and uses them to stir the cream into his coffee. "But those plastic stirs are so wasteful."

I think about how I change my tampon in my car sometimes and then forget the old one in my cupholder. "That's not the grossest thing I've seen," I reply as I grab a plastic stir anyway and mix my coffee.

We take our coffees and head back to the car. We spend the next seven hours hiking, talking and continually coming up with reasons to spend "just a few more minutes" together.

I fall hard. He is everything that none of the people I've dated have ever been. He is funny and witty in a way that I have never been matched with before. We have a constant push-pull of giving each other a hard time while also ensuring that the other knows how we really feel. I can feel that neither of us need the other. We simply witness each other without wanting to judge or change anything. It is exciting and nerve-wracking and comforting and secure all at once—a combination I didn't even know was possible.

"So, when do we make this 'official?'" Bryan prods as he drives us home from a wedding we just attended together. I play another song from my "romantic playlist" and pretend like I didn't pre-plan the music at all.

"Honestly, I don't know," I say, "and I don't know what will happen." I continue. "But I know that if I've learned anything from you, it's that all of my other relationships weren't real," I say without fear. I hold his hand and glance over. He's smiling.

And they weren't real. None of my previous relationships were real because I never allowed them to be. Even during my six-year relationship with Ben, there was a large part of myself that I withheld from him. Although Bryan was a part of the reason I felt so incredible, the real reason I was experiencing the type of love I always wanted was because I was allowing myself to. For the first time in my entire life, I allowed myself to be vulnerable, to be seen, and to truly love and be loved in return.

Wow, I think as I lay on my couch and check in with everything I've been feeling. *I guess this is just how you feel when you meet the right person,* I think. But another thought pops into my head. *No, this is what it feels like when you allow yourself to fully love.*

One of the craziest parts of this relationship is that the more I allow myself to love Bryan, the more deeply I connect with my own self-love. This deeper self-love is available to me because I finally stopped telling myself that my true self was unlovable by hiding and playing games. Everytime I felt vulnerable and chose to love through that vulnerability, I sent a new message to myself, "My true self is perfect and able to give and receive all the love I desire."

I am all in. When my fear tells me to play hard to get, I connect with Bryan instead. When my fear tells me to hide a part of who I am, I reveal it loudly and vibrantly. When I am afraid to express my feelings, I freaking recite poetry-like truths about how I feel about him. I am saying shit to my friends like, "I have never felt seen the way I feel seen by Bryan," and although it is probably super obnoxious to listen to, it's true. I am allowing myself to be seen, I am allowing myself to love, and I am opening myself up to the gaping, raw, tornado of fear and discomfort that is being 100% vulnerable while waiting to see if your love is returned.

In the end, mine wasn't returned. But as I waited for the insurmountable pain I had always imagined would swallow me whole after being so vulnerable and experiencing rejection, it didn't arrive. Did I feel hurt? Of course. Did it suck? Yes. But I also felt freaking awesome! I didn't have to wonder if things would have worked out if I had been nicer, more open, or more true to myself. I didn't have to look back and realize all the ways I sabotaged the relationship because of fear. Being vulnerable allowed me to be my fun, loving, true self because I wasn't consumed by the fear of being hurt. Not only that, but being vulnerable also allowed me to be more attentive and caring toward my partner. The relationship ending had nothing to do with me being vulnerable and showing my true self. It ended because we both had a little more healing work to do. Bryan had his own unhealed wounds surrounding unhealthy love that affected his ability to receive my love. And, if I'm being honest, for as vulnerable as I felt – and had truly been – I still had many layers of guardedness that I needed to recognize and let down.

When the relationship ended, I spiraled into the belief that I had once again recreated my past and that all the self-work I had done was just an illusion. I thought that the relationship ending was a sign that I wasn't truly healed—that all the years I spent wading through the grueling pain involved in self-work, shedding bullshit thoughts, re-learning new truths, identifying and healing voids, caring for wounds, and figuring out what the fuck healthy love was hadn't worked. I thought that this failed relationship meant that I wasn't actually as whole, conscious, or healed as I thought. (Not the best example of self-love.)

"Okay, so how did I recreate my past this time?" I say out loud. "What giant red flags did I ignore and what bullshit did I accept because of unhealed wounds from my past?" I sarcastically ask as I wait for a floodgate of truths and regrets to burst open and soak me.

My friend rolls her eyes at the unnecessary drama. "You're always talking about lessons," she says. "What do you think the lesson for this relationship is?"

I think about it. Again, I'm looking for the giant blindspot to reveal itself—the "This time, you managed to date a combination of both your fucked up father and mother. Congrats for learning. Better luck next time!"

I prepare for defeat as I wait for the lesson to reveal itself.

Then, it hits me. "That I can do it," I say shocked. I'm a little more excited now as I continue, "I was supposed to learn that I can do it. I can be vulnerable and not let all my shit from the past sabotage the love that I want." I'm pumped now, "I can love truly and deeply and be loved truly and deeply in return without losing myself... holy shit!" I burst with excitement. "That was the whole point!"

No, the relationship didn't work out, but I never needed the relationship to validate the fact that I had grown exponentially. I now know that I am capable of giving and allowing myself to receive all the healthy love I've always dreamed of. I can give space to another person without giving up who I am—bring on the scrambled eggs recipe, I ain't scared anymore! I now understand the balance between setting healthy boundaries and staying true to myself while also being vulnerable and allowing someone into my life. I'm also capable of identifying when a partner isn't right for me, and letting him go instead of holding on in order to fill voids. I can show every part of who I am to another person. I can be vulnerable. I can do it! And when I do find my match, this vulnerability is going to make for some real, enlightened AF, magical love.

My friend continues to drive as we approach a coffee shop.

"Let me grab a coffee," I say to my friend. She pulls over and I run into the shop. I order my medium decaf and walk over to the half and half station. I add my cream and reach for a plastic stir, but stop.

"The plastic stirs are wasteful," I say to a bystander who doesn't care. I smile, grab my keys, and begin stirring.

Putting It All Together and Letting Yourself Love

So how do you let someone in? My point in sharing these stories with you is to 1.) laugh a little, 2.) hopefully inspire you to lovingly reflect on your own relationship journeys, and 3.) discuss significant realizations that each relationship revealed. Just as Eckhart Tolle describes at the beginning of this chapter, relationships are one of the most powerful tools for aligning with our true selves and callings.

So, how the heck do you open up to someone? Here are some tips I've gathered along my nine years of relationship journeys.

Think About the *Lessons* You've Learned

I truly believe that every person we meet has a message for us, and it's up to us to allow ourselves to receive that message. Relationships are a perfect example of this. Each of my relationship journeys have offered some of the greatest tools for becoming conscious of all the ways my past was keeping me from fully loving myself and from allowing myself to love and be loved in return. Sometimes my relationships offered beautiful lessons about self-love or the safety that exists in vulnerability. Other times, these relationships painfully illuminated bullshit beliefs that I needed to unlearn or voids that I needed to heal. Regardless, recognizing these lessons has been a significant tool in healing and learning to truly love. Take some time to reflect on the lessons you have learned from your relationship journeys.

Identify Your *Games*

What is your go-to game? For me, it was making a guy long for me but never letting him have me. Maybe your game is wanting what you can't have, so you play all the games, but as soon as you start connecting with the person, you lose interest. Perhaps your game is to remove yourself from the game completely—to shut yourself off from connecting with others in order to protect yourself from being hurt. Perhaps your game involves saving people—always offering healing love to partners who can't love themselves as a way to position yourself as a "savior." You believe that this savior status will position you as someone your partner needs and loves deeply. This way, you'll never have to worry about them leaving. We all have a game that we're playing, even if we don't mean to. Take some time to identify your game.

Recognize What You're Using Your Game to *Protect* Yourself From

My game was to make a man "long for me but never have me." This was my game because I had a deep fear of abandonment. When a man longed for me, I could feel his desire, I felt wanted, I felt beautiful, sexy and admired, but I never had to deal with all the gut-wrenching emotions that would develop if I fell in love with him, or the fear of him leaving.

If your game is wanting what you can't have, or loving the "chase" of a new relationship but becoming bored once you're committed, you are probably afraid of engulfment. As a trauma survivor, you never learned what healthy love felt like. Instead, you learned that love was an elusive concept that you had to constantly chase but never actually receive. Now, once the partner you've been adamantly pursuing commits to you, you have to deal with all the uncomfortable fears and beliefs associated with feeling controlled, trapped, suffocated, or bored by the relationship.

Many times, our fears are based in a combination of both abandonment and engulfment. I would play games for months with a guy before accepting a date, which was a way to test if he was truly committed to dating me (easing my fear of abandonment). Once we were in a relationship and he began wanting to spend more time with me, I was terrified of losing myself in the relationship and began pulling away or resenting my partner (fear of engulfment).

Once you know what your game is, take some time to identify what you subconsciously feel that game is protecting you from.

Start Small

Believe me, I didn't start by recognizing that my fear of embracing my boyfriend's scrambled egg recipe was a sign of my fear of engulfment. I started small. I started by allowing my partner into my life in ways that, to most people, probably seemed incredibly insignificant but were huge steps for me. I added a photo of us to his contact in my phone - something I had never done before in my life. When he suggested a way to hang my clothes so that they dried more quickly, I tried it without fearing that I was losing myself by doing so. There was a moment when a group of my friends and I were talking about guys and, normally, I would have started talking about how big I hoped Bryan's dick was when we did start having sex. It would have been a way for me to publically detach any feelings I had toward him and position him as simply an object I was eventually going have sex with and not care about later. It would have been a way for me to protect myself from the vulnerability that came with how much I really did like him. I stopped myself. I respected him. I liked him, and the idea of talking so disrespectfully about him sucked. So, I didn't.

Start small. Do all the little things you would normally avoid to prevent yourself from connecting with a partner. Those are the things that lay the foundation of vulnerability. With every small step you take, you will feel more confident in your ability to keep connecting without getting hurt.

Have Your Binoculars Ready

Shit is going to come out. Especially when you are on a roll of healthy decision-making and you are really connecting with your partner, your ego is going to do anything it possibly can to convince you to freak out. And it's not your fault. Your ego has spent the majority of your life trying to protect you from ever being hurt the way you were during the abuse, so witnessing you allowing yourself to be open to love is going to terrify your ego.

Get your binoculars ready so you can spot all the negative beliefs, old patterns, and unhealthy habits running in from miles away. Seriously though, identify when patterns are starting to creep back in. A great way to tell that your ego is on overdrive is when you are super, super happy and secure in your relationship one day, then a day later you're like, "I cannot possibly be this happy forever, something has to go wrong." A little seed of doubt creeps in and an hour later that seed has grown into full blown "this person has no interest in me and our relationship is over because he said he would call at eight and it's 8:02." The type of love you want is going to take work. It took SO MUCH work for me to identify old patterns while I was in a relationship with Bryan. But that work is also incredibly rewarding when you commit to it.

Be *Gentle* With Yourself

There are going to be times when you slip up—when you start a stupid argument with your partner because things have been going great and you're used to chaos. There are going to be times when your partner runs into his ex and you have an intense urge to flirt with someone in front of him to make him jealous so that you're not the only one feeling insecure. You are going to do stupid shit sometimes. It's okay. Don't make it a habit, but don't beat yourself up either. Simply take responsibility for your actions, and then move forward healthily from a place of awareness.

Love Yourself

EVERYTHING starts here, my friend. So make sure this relationship has strong foundations before you enter into one with someone else. The only reason I was able to love Bryan as vulnerably as I did was because I truly loved myself and could remind myself that allowing myself to be vulnerable and love someone is also an act of self-love. When you allow yourself to be vulnerable, you are telling yourself that you don't have to hide any parts of yourself, you know you are whole, and that you deserve to give and receive all the love you desire.

Talk to Your Partner
About Your Past

"I need to tell you something," I say to a friend who has been asking me out repeatedly. It's loud, we're at a frat party, and me and this friend just grabbed another beer. I've been anxiously holding back from this conversation but I can't hold it in anymore, so I decide that between the keg and the pool table at this fraternity is as good a place as any.

"We've been friends for a while and I know you want to date," I say, "but before we do, I need to tell you something."

"Okay," he casually responds as he takes a swig of his beer.

"Okay," I say as I prepare myself to continue. "I was sexually abused by both of my parents," I say as quickly as I can. "And because of that, sometimes, dating can be hard."

He shifts positions and takes another drink. "That's what she said," he responds. "...Because you said 'it's hard sometimes,'" he continues as he nervously laughs and looks away from me.

Yes, he really said that. Now, I will be the first to admit that my timing isn't always the greatest when it comes to choosing a moment to have serious conversations. Regardless, his response was freaking stupid, and unsupportive, unkind, heartless, immature, but I'll just use "freaking stupid" as an umbrella term.

I don't share this story to scare you. I want to encourage you to share your story *when you're ready*, but I just want to take a second to acknowledge that you may get some freaking stupid responses when you share your story. Let's recognize that these responses have nothing to do with us and everything to do with the other person's emotional ineptitude. Laugh about them, then move forward.

As you know, deeply connecting with someone in a truly loving capacity requires truth and vulnerability, which, if you're thinking about sharing your past with a partner, you've obviously successfully allowed yourself to be vulnerable and connect with someone. So, let's start by taking a second to celebrate that!

Real love requires you to share all of yourself with another person and allow the other to do the same. This sharing is what makes real relationships so beautiful and special, but it's also what sometimes makes talking with a partner about the past intimidating. I have no problem openly talking about my experiences of abuse—I mean, my entire life purpose involves sharing my stories with large groups of people I don't yet know. But when it comes to talking with my partner for the first time about the abuse, I still get a little nervous. Granted, now I have the internet and an entire book to kind of ease him into the conversation, but before that, I had to learn how to allow a partner to hold space for me during this conversation. Here are a few things I learned:

Talk About It When You Want To

During my first relationship, it was very important for me to talk to Ben about the abuse I experienced before we had sex. He was the first man I was going to have sex with, and I needed to feel connected with him and know that he could respectfully and lovingly hold that part of my past. When I dated Steve, I told him immediately about the abuse I experienced because I was recreating my past by playing the victim role and seeking sympathy. After Steve, I hooked up with a guy I met on a dating app. All I wanted was to have sex. I didn't want any part of my past to have anything to do with it, so I never told him.

When I met Bryan, I knew that I wanted to connect with him in a way that made us both feel safe sharing our pasts. But I had also done a lot of my own work and healing so I was no longer playing a victim role or looking for someone to heal those wounds for me. As a result, I took my time getting to know him. I took my time feeling out the relationship. I took my time revealing parts of myself and talking with him about my past.

My point is there is no right or wrong time to have the conversation. Simply do it when you feel comfortable, respected, and safe.

Meditate About It Beforehand

For many years, I only thought about what I wanted to say to my partner. I had the script written, I probably planned when and where I wanted to have the conversation. After a while, I realized that all of this preparation was actually for him, not for me. I was so worried that he would feel uncomfortable during the conversation that I put tons of energy into planning ways to make him feel better. None of that prep-work focused on my needs.

Take time to meditate before your conversation with your partner about the most important aspects of this conversation: What do you want from this conversation? How do you want to feel? What do you need from your partner during this conversation?

Be Clear About What You Need

I am going to be entirely honest - none of my partners have ever met my expectations for this conversation. That was partly on them, but it was also largely on me. I set incredibly high expectations for this conversation and I based my desire to continue with the relationship almost entirely on how they responded. I wanted him to say all the right things, I wanted him to make me feel a certain way (something no one can ever actually do), I wanted him to have the absolute perfect reaction. When he didn't do all of those things, I resented him. One day I thought, *Why isn't he reacting the way I want him to? I want him to...* Then I stopped. I realized that I had never actually decided exactly what I needed from him at that moment. The expectations I set for my partner were impossible to meet because I didn't even know, for myself, exactly what I needed from him.

Maybe you need your partner to hold you close and pet your head. Maybe you need your partner to get angry for you. Maybe you need your partner to simply listen. Maybe you need your partner to express empathy and understanding. Whatever it is that you need from your partner is perfect. You simply need to know what it is. So get clear about it.

Once you know what you need, communicate it clearly and directly. It can be as simple as, "[insert name], I want to talk to you about something that is really important to me, but it's a very vulnerable topic for me. So, in order to feel cared for and heard, I would really love for you to hold me while I talk/reflect back to me the emotions you hear me state/not say anything until I've finished what I have to say." This is you loving yourself by setting boundaries and making your needs known. This conversation also allows your partner the opportunity to respond to your needs and to connect with you during a very vulnerable moment in your relationship.

That said, not everyone will be able to meet your needs, which brings me to my next point.

Not Everyone Will Say the Right Things

Although I may get nervous while having this conversation with my partner, simply articulating that I've experienced abuse is not difficult for me. I have done it hundreds of times in my life. My entire career is built around being open about abuse so the topic of sexual assault is not shocking to me. But it is shocking for a lot of people. I didn't understand that for a long time, and I was often hurt by the speechlessness of my partners—something I interpreted as a lack of empathy.

Now, I am not making excuses for anyone. Some people will genuinely have bad reactions. But there are some people who are simply not going to know what to say at that moment, or empathizing and articulating deep emotions is not a skill they possess. At that time, you can choose to help them by telling them something they could say that would be helpful to you, or you could give them some time to process what you told them and talk about it later, or you can accept that they may not be capable of providing support in the way that you want them to and ask them to support you in a way they feel most comfortable. Whatever you decide, make sure that it's something that helps you both feel respected and heard.

Some People Will React Poorly

See "That's what she said" guy. The only thing that you need to know about these people is that their reactions have nothing to do with you. I repeat: anyone's poor reaction to your story has nothing to do with you and everything to do with their own shit. I know a friend who shared her story of childhood sexual abuse with a partner and the man responded,

"So, does this mean you're into weird, kinky sex?" Those people have their own healing to do. Please do not take on the feelings they put towards you or your story. Instead, recognize that they are incapable of reacting in a loving manner and let them go. You have done the most courageous and beautiful things a human can do - you allowed yourself to be vulnerable and offered someone the opportunity to connect with you. Please be proud of yourself and do not allow this person's reaction to keep you from connecting with others in the future.

Focus on How You Feel

There are going to be a lot of feelings swirling around during this conversation: vulnerability, connection, fear, love, relief, etc. Try to take a few moments to sort through all those emotions and focus on how you feel about this conversation. Do you feel satisfied? Is there more you want to say? Do you feel disappointed? Do you feel hurt? You don't have to find solutions to your emotions at that moment. Simply take note of your true feelings.

If You Feel Supported, Let Your Partner Know

This is also a vulnerable conversation for your partner. If you are at the stage in your relationship where you feel close enough to have this conversation, your partner probably cares for you deeply and wants to respond in a way that makes you feel cared for. If you do feel supported and loved, let them know. Thank them for their support and let them know that you will be there for them during any difficult conversations as well.

Love Yourself

Woo! You did it! Take a deep breath in and out, and celebrate yourself.

So we've had our initial conversation about abuse, but what happens after that? How do we deal with the everyday conversations that may pop up along the way? I'm so glad you asked!

You Will Be Triggered Sometimes

There are going to be times when something seemingly so simple that your partner says will trigger a very strong emotional response for you. Maybe you'll be having a casual conversation about tomatoes when he says something that makes you suddenly think, *What the fuck did he mean by that?*

Maybe you'll suddenly feel hurt or angry or betrayed or insecure. Most of the time, our first reaction is to immediately launch into defense mode and react with a hurtful comment or action. This, in turn, activates our partner's defense mode and she/he says something that furthers our defense. This continues back and forth until we have both hurt each other for reasons we don't even understand.

My absolute number one piece of advice in this situation is to ask yourself, "Is this feeling the truth or the past? Am I experiencing this amount of anger because of something my partner said to actually invoke that anger or did his/her comment just poke a really raw part of my past?" I recognize that, in the moment, it's not always easy to do this because emotions can feel all-consuming. But I can promise that if you react to these emotions without taking the time to reflect on them and decipher what is and isn't the truth, you will eventually sabotage the relationship. The easiest way to take some time to reflect is to say to your partner, "Oh, some past stuff just popped up and I am feeling very [insert emotion]. Let me take a second to think about all of this." Boom. Now your partner understands that you're feeling a certain way without feeling attacked for no reason. You have set the boundary that you need time to think and you gave your partner the opportunity to understand what you're experiencing instead of simply being hurt by a reaction.

Write It Down

There are many times that I do not understand the feeling I am experiencing at the moment, or I am not sure exactly how I want to share a memory with a partner. If I have the opportunity, I take the time to write down what I want to say. Writing has always been a beautiful tool for working through my experiences and emotions. Writing things down beforehand gives me the opportunity to work things out for myself first, and figure out how I want to articulate things before I talk with my partner. If writing isn't your thing, try singing what you want to say in the shower, or painting it, or any other method of expressing yourself that you feel most comfortable using.

Love Yourself

Just wanted to remind you again. Celebrate yourself. You may feel vulnerable, but it's an incredibly powerful thing to allow someone to hold space for your past.

Know Who
You Are

I am in first grade, and me and my sister share a bed. I look over at my sister, but she is turned away from me. Lisa gets up from our bed and walks to the door of my room. She turns and, before closing the door, smiles and waves. As soon as the door closes, I begin crying. I try to look at my sister again, but she isn't moving. She is barely breathing. I can tell that she's left the same way that I do during the abuse. I can't feel her energy with me because she is gone.

"I'm sorry," I whisper quietly between tears. I lay on my back on my side of the bed. Lisa just forced me to sexually abuse my sister. Lisa and Tim frequently force us to abuse each other. I hate myself. I am a monster. The thought of hurting my sister makes me want to die, but I did it and I am still forced to live. I want to sleep, but I can't. I know that the abuse isn't over. I know that as soon as I close my eyes and begin to sleep, Tim will enter our room and there will be more abuse. All I can do is cry.

I look out the window and notice that the moon is full and really bright. The whole room is illuminated by its light. For a second, I am distracted.

I know there's more. I am not this. I am not what's happening. I am not this life. I know there is more and I am going to find it. I am going to live it. I am only in first grade, so I don't actually think any of this, but as I look at the moon, I can feel it. For a second, I feel calm. I can't escape right now. I can't take back anything that has happened. But somehow, I feel that I am okay. I am okay now and I will be okay in the future.

I hold my own hand to try and comfort myself. I gently place one hand into the other and squeeze. Eventually, I fall asleep.

Many people have asked me how I was able to survive the abuse and come out so well adjusted. Many survivors of abuse meet a teacher or a friend's parent, or a neighbor they can confide in and who helps them escape the abuse. I never had that, and that amazes a lot of people. "How were you able to do it?" they ask. For a long time, whenever someone asked me that question, a very distinct feeling would pop up, but I could never describe it. The closest I could ever get to describing this feeling was to say, "I just always knew that everything would be okay." But that description didn't suffice. It wasn't until I read Eckhart Tolle's book, *The Power of Now*, that I finally understood the feeling that carried me through all those years of abuse.

We have two parts: There is the part of ourselves that is consumed by thought. We'll call this side of ourselves the Ego. The Ego always has something to worry about, to criticize, to keep us thinking about - either the past or the future - and, in doing so, it always inhibits us from living in the present. Then there is our true being, I am going to call this part of ourselves our Soul. This is the side of us we feel when we are truly present. This is the part of ourselves that knows that we aren't our physical bodies or our life circumstances, or our jobs, or relationships, or material possessions. We simply are, and we will be when all of those other things, or people, or places no longer exist. This is the part of ourselves where peace and safety and calm always exist. This is the part of ourselves that we experience when we wake up on a winter morning, open our windows and are taken aback by the beauty of a snow-covered backyard. For just a moment, our brains shut off, we're no longer thinking. We are simply existing in the present moment along with the beauty of the natural world.

This peace and calm and safety exist within us every second of every day, but we rarely access it because we can't shut off our Egos. We can't stop thinking. When do you feel most connected to yourself? Maybe it's during a meditation or a yoga class. Maybe it's while you're running that grueling marathon. I know a lot of people who feel most free and connected to themselves when they are doing something dangerous. Why? Because it is in those moments of danger that your brain has to shut off. You can't think about what you're going to have for breakfast tomorrow or whether or not you'll lose your job while you're jumping out of an airplane. In those moments of danger, you either focus on the present moment or you die. Now, I am not suggesting that you jump out of a plane in order to experience your true self. But all of us want to feel that connection to our true selves, we just don't know how. I will talk about a few ways to connect with our Souls in a moment. But first, I want to dive a little deeper into knowing who you are.

As I held my own hand, I knew, without a doubt, that everything was going to be okay. Not only that, but I knew in that moment that I was okay. How is that possible?

For a long time, as I looked back on that moment, I imagined myself disconnected from my body. I always attributed that feeling with having dissociated to get through it. But as I dove deeper into the memory, I realized that I wasn't detached from my body. I detached from the situation. I completely disconnected myself from all of the circumstances - the horrifying acts that had just occurred, the nightmare I was living, the abusive parents, the emotions I was experiencing, the fear - I took a step back from all of it because I knew that none of it was me. Most importantly, I knew that none of it could affect who I truly was—my true being, my Soul. My Soul can never be hurt. It can never be destroyed. It is the ever-present core of who I am.

A few years ago, I attended a women's retreat during which I participated in a meditation where we discovered our "inner landscapes." During that meditation, I saw myself on a beach, laughing. I started crying because I hadn't seen myself that happy in years. After the meditation, we gathered in small groups to talk about what we had experienced. I told my group that I had seen myself laughing. The group leader turned to me, held my hand, and said, "That means that you are okay. Your true self is okay." I cried again because until that moment, after everything I had experienced, I hadn't really been sure that all of me was okay. The laughing woman I saw on the beach that day is my Soul—she's my true being. She is the part of myself who laughs at sadness for the past or concern for the future. She laughs when things are going wrong at work or when a relationship is ending because she can never be hurt or destroyed by any of it. I can never be truly hurt or destroyed by any of it.

By some gift from the Universe, I was given the ability to understand that there was a part of me far deeper than my circumstances in life. I understood that no matter how hard someone tried to destroy who I was on the outside, they could never destroy my Soul. They could never destroy *me*. That is how I was able to survive the abuse. You have the power to do the same.

Observe Your Thoughts

You are not your emotions. You are not your thoughts. This is something that most of us don't even realize, which is why our lives can feel so overwhelming. When something stressful happens and our brains start spiraling into a storm of *what ifs* and *whys*, when the anger or worry or sadness starts filtering in and we're suddenly consumed by emotions, it is very difficult to remember that thoughts and emotions are both things we experience—they are not who we are. This is an incredibly difficult concept to grasp because it's so simple. When you are experiencing anger, are you anger? No, you feel angry, but you, yourself, are not anger. So why do you let it consume you?

Stop Time Traveling

When you find out your workplace is laying people off, you start imagining being fired. You start thinking about all the work you've put into this company, analyzing every moment of the past you've spent there. You feel angry. You start imagining telling your boss about all of that work. You imagine her not caring, which gets you even more upset.

Now, you start thinking about all of the things you may have overlooked at your job. You feel remorse. You suddenly realize that you'll have to find a new job. So now, you're re-living the past while also living out a fake future conversation with your boss while imagining the job search you are about to embark on.

You're time traveling and it's freaking exhausting. Stop doing it. When your brain wants to pull you into a dark abyss full of analyzing the past and predicting the future, just stop and observe.

Be Still

This is the hardest task for me, and I'm guessing for most people. Why do you think so few people meditate? Because if it were easy, everyone would be doing it. But sitting with yourself and trying to quiet your racing mind is difficult. Do it anyways. I set a timer for five minutes, and during those five minutes, I take three deep breaths. As I inhale, I say, "In with the present moment," and as I exhale, I say, "Out with everything else." Then I let stillness and darkness completely take over. Your mind will wander. When that happens, just gently call it out. I say, "Wow, my mind is wandering today." Simply calling attention to the fact that you are having trouble focusing brings you right back into the present moment. You may feel antsy the first couple times you try. But I guarantee, after those five minutes, you will feel refreshed because you just let go of all the bullshit that doesn't matter and you connected with your true self, your Soul.

Recognize Your True Self

We have all felt our true selves. We just, for whatever reason, don't believe that we are strong enough to feel that intensely connected with ourselves all the time. We also let the craziness of everyday life distract us from our true selves. But the truth is, we are always our true selves, so we can always access her. So, know who you are. When the bullshit thoughts start running through your head, stop and say, "I know who I am." When work or relationships or traffic jams have you on the brink of a meltdown, know who you are. You are, have always been, and will always be far more powerful than any temporary life situation. And every life situation is just that, temporary. Your true being is the only indestructible force on the planet.

Love Yourself

For a long time, I thought that I had to be cured. I needed to cure the pain I felt about the abuse. I needed to cure the way I lived my life after the abuse. But my experiences aren't a disease that is crippling me. In fact, it's the opposite. My experiences are a huge part of why I am me. I struggle with dissociation and sometimes that leaves me disconnected from my body and the people around me. But dissociation also allows me to take a step back from the circumstances of my life and observe the situation before I act, and that is a really powerful life skill.

Sometimes I struggle to be sexually intimate, but that has positioned sex as something that I reserve for people I feel truly connected and safe with, and that's a beautiful thing. Sometimes my wanting a family void is so overwhelming that it feels like it might swallow me whole. But that same void is what has taught me to never take my loved ones for granted and to never miss a moment to show the people around me that I love them. For every struggle I perceive myself as having to cure or erase, there is an underlying beauty and key piece to who I am. Love yourself and recognize that beauty.

Your Turn

I am going to be very honest with you. I stopped going to events for sexual assault survivors a long time ago. And for a while, I felt guilty about it. How could I claim to be all for empowering people who have experienced trauma when I don't go to events for trauma survivors? The answer was a little harsh but simple, "Because I feel depressed AF during those events."

The first time I attended an event for survivors, I felt incredibly empowered. I shared my story out loud and was immediately supported by a group of people who, in their own way, understood exactly how I was feeling. Simply having a supportive space to tell my story out loud was incredibly empowering. But as I continued to attend these events, the experience turned from empowering to depressing. I was sharing the same stories over and over again and I no longer felt powerful doing so. Instead, I felt stuck - stuck in the past and stuck in my old stories. *What's next?* I thought. I wanted to talk about more than just my memories of abuse. I wanted to talk about how to work through my fear of intimacy so that I could hold someone's hand. I wanted to talk about how to work through triggers so that I could touch my own body in the shower. I wanted to talk about how to stop looking for safety in other people and things. I wanted to talk about my life outside of the abuse, and I needed a new conversation to do that.

I have shared a lot in this book. Like, a lot, a lot. Like, I shared my masurbation journey with you a lot. Some may call this oversharing, but I think it's necessary. For a long time, I thought that I was the only person struggling to hold someone's hand or touch myself in the shower or find safety within myself. I thought I was the only one because no one ever talked about any of these topics. No one ever talked about these topics not because they didn't want to, but because they didn't know how. The reason we only talked about our abuse stories during events was because no one is teaching us how to have other types of conversations about trauma.

My first mission in creating this book was to share as much as I possibly could so that you know that you are not alone in any of your experiences. And if you're experiencing something that I didn't mention in this book, I guarantee that there is someone else in this world who is experiencing the same thing. But there is more to my mission than simply sharing and connecting through experiences. I want this new type of conversation about trauma to become the norm. I want every single person who has ever experienced trauma to feel comfortable sharing their stories and asking questions so that they can truly grow, heal, and live beyond the trauma. That's where you come in.

I've shared my story. I've started the conversation. Now, it's your turn. I've shared countless tools with you to help you navigate your own experiences. Now, you have the opportunity to not only continue to grow for yourself, but to help others do the same. There is someone out there feeling alone, scared, and stuck in the same ways that you've felt, but they'll never know how to talk about it unless you show them. Share your story, hold community workshops using the tools provided in this book, host new events for survivors, yell from the rooftops - do it however fuels your soul, just make sure you have these conversations. The next time you're talking to someone who's working through abuse, say, "Hey, I know how you're feeling. Try doing this and see if it helps…" Then get some cake pops and coffee and share some stories.

About the Author

As an author, speaker, and trauma survivor coach, Katie is deeply passionate about oversharing. Her mission is to share her very real (and frequently awkward) stories of navigating healing from eighteen years of childhood sexual abuse so that others feel comfortable laughing about, loving, and sharing their own stories.

When Katie first started working through the abuse, she looked to books for guidance on how to talk about her experiences. But all she could find were psychology books or heavily titled self-help books that made her feel like the vastness of her shit was insurmountable. No one talked about the other parts of her story - all the parts that included the beautiful, lighthearted, meaningful, funny, significant moments in her life. She wanted a different kind of conversation about sexual abuse. Katie's debut book, *Cake Pops and Coffee*, is that new type of conversation.

In her book and in her work, Katie gets very real about the whole story of trauma - the difficult and the beautiful. She talks about how she made herself small and sabotaged her success because of negative beliefs that caused her to be afraid of being seen. She talks about saving her past selves and learning how to find safety within herself. She shares how she learned to masturbate in a way that transformed her perception of pleasure and allowed her to connect with her partner during intimacy. She talks about navigating relationships and sharing her past with the people she loves. She shares how she cut through all the bullshit that resulted from the abuse and how she learned to step into her power, love herself on a deeper level, and truly live after trauma - all while sharing tips and guidance on how you can do the same.

Katie's tips have been featured in *Painted Magazine* and Live Fervently Podcast, an inspirational podcast for game-changing women. One reader described *Cake Pops and Coffee* as "she has managed to write a book that discusses some of the heaviest things I've ever heard while also being really funny and inviting. I just can't get over that because I need you to understand how much skill it takes to accomplish that!"

Katie is changing the way we talk about sexual assault. She believes that we can have conversations about trauma with laughter and approachability instead of heaviness and discomfort, all while feeling supported and safe. So, grab some cake pops and coffee and get ready to share some stories.

KATIEMALONEYCOACHING.COM

Made in the USA
Monee, IL
10 May 2020